THE LAST TRAIN

A HOLOCAUST STORY

BY RONA ARATO

Owl
kids

Owlkids Books acknowledges the financial support of the Canada Council for the Arts, the Ontario Arts Council, the Government of Canada through the Canada Book Fund (CBF) and the Government of Ontario through the Ontario Creates Book Initiative for our publishing activities.

Published in Canada by
Owlkids Books Inc.
1 Eglinton Avenue East
Toronto, ON M4P 3A1

Published in the United States by
Owlkids Books Inc.
1700 Fourth Street
Berkeley, CA 94710

Cataloguing data available from Library and Archives Canada

ISBN 978-1-926973-62-3 (HC)
978-1-926973-71-5 (ePUB); 978-1-77147-396-5 (PB)

Library of Congress Control Number: 2012945654

Edited by John Crossingham
Designed by Barb Kelly

Manufactured in Altona, MB, Canada, in March 2019, by Friesens Corporation
Job #252838

E   F   G   H   I   J

Publisher of Chirp, Chickadee and OWL
www.owlkidsbooks.com

Owlkids Books is a division of

For my husband, Paul,
and in memory of his brother, Oscar,
and their beloved parents,
Lenke and Ignaz

Introduction

My name is Rona Arato. My husband, Paul, was a survivor of the Holocaust that occurred during the Second World War. I knew some of Paul's story: he, his brother, Oscar, and their mother, Lenke, were in the Bergen Belsen Concentration Camp and on a death train that was liberated by the American Ninth Army. But many of the details from that awful time were missing. It was only after we learned about the Teaching History Matters project and met other train survivors and the soldiers who liberated them that we were really able to put the pieces of his story together.

To tell it, I listened to many testimonies and read the memoirs of the survivors and soldiers from that fateful event and the camp. Matt Rozell—the teacher who created Teaching History Matters and brought us all together—and the historians at the Bergen Belsen Memorial were all generous with information. In 1994, Paul and I attended a memorial service in the Karcagi Synagogue commemorating the 50th anniversary of the German occupation, and I had the opportunity then, and on subsequent trips, to get to know the people who appear as children in this book.

What you read here is all based on actual events. I have tried to honor the integrity and truth of everyone's story. The dialogue is mostly imagined, but the account it tells is true. The main characters are real people.

This has been a difficult book to write but one that I knew I had to write. It is a tribute to the train survivors, the soldiers who liberated them, and to Matt Rozell.

Rona Arato

Prologue
Toronto, Canada
Spring 2008

The picture on the computer screen shows a woman running toward the camera, arms outstretched, her face a mask of surprise. Yet what catches Paul's attention is in the backdrop—an abandoned freight train. Sixty years earlier he was on that train. He was six years old on April 13, 1945, when two American soldiers in a tank liberated him, his mother, his brother, and thousands of other prisoners. For sixty years he has thought about that day and about the soldiers who saved their lives.

Chapter 1

Karcag, Hungary
April 1944

Ma nishtana ha-laila ha-zeh mi-kol ha-lelot? Why is this night different from all other nights?

This night is different because our fathers are not with us.

Paul listened to the familiar words of the Four Questions, the heart of the Passover Seder.

This night is different because we are celebrating Passover without our fathers.

He looked around the synagogue social hall, where women, children, and a few elderly men sat at tables draped with white cloth. Paul thought of Passovers he and his older brother, Oscar, spent at their grandparents' house, when all his aunts, uncles, and cousins were still together. But his father, like other men in town, had been taken away to some kind of work camp, so his mother and some other women had organized this Seder to celebrate Passover, the holiday of freedom. And tonight, as they recited prayers, sang familiar melodies, and ate matzo (unleavened bread), chicken soup, and roast chicken, they tried to forget, for a few hours, about the missing fathers, brothers, and grandfathers, and this thing called war raging around them.

The next day, the Germans marched into Karcag.

Chapter 2

Oscar and Paul watched from a dusty street corner as trucks rumbled by. Tall men with guns slung over their shoulders stepped past them. Their faces were hard; their eyes looked straight ahead. Wide-eyed, Paul munched on a piece of matzo as they passed.

"Oscar, who are they?" Paul asked.

"Soldiers."

"They look mean. I don't like them."

Oscar cupped Paul's mouth. "Don't let them hear you say that."

"Why not?"

"Because they might get angry." With his blue eyes and fair skin, Oscar resembled their father, while Paul's black curly hair and brown eyes were like their mother's. Oscar bent down so that his head was level with his brother's. "Don't ask questions," he said. "Just listen to me."

"Yes, Oscar, *sir*." Paul grinned. "But I still don't like them."

Oscar sighed. Paul was pretty smart, but he liked to do things his own way. As the older brother, it was ten-year-old Oscar's job to watch out for his five-year-old brother. When their father left, he put Oscar in charge of keeping Paul safe.

Apu told me to keep Paul out of fights and make sure he

doesn't upset our mother. So it's my job to keep him out of trouble with the soldiers.

Suddenly, a hand grasped Oscar's shoulder. He jumped.

"*Anyu!* You scared me."

"Come home," she said, her voice trembling. "Come! Now!"

Oscar looked into his mother's eyes and saw fear.

✡ ✡ ✡

As they walked home, Oscar looked sadly at his mother. Fear was new to him. He had lived his whole life in Karcag. It was a small town and he knew every part of it, from the muddy street where his family lived to the town square, which was paved with cobblestones and surrounded by shops. There was a Catholic Church, a Protestant church, and a synagogue. He and Paul attended the Jewish school, next to the synagogue. On the surface, everyone seemed to get along, but Oscar knew, from what he'd overheard, that the Jews always felt like outsiders. *And that's what our name means,* he thought. His father had told him that *Auslander* was a German word that meant foreigner.

"To the Hungarians we will always be Jews first and Hungarian second—if at all," his father had said. "I can only teach Jewish children and the Jewish doctor can only see Jewish patients. But the others leave us alone, and we leave them alone, and that way we all get along."

Not anymore, Oscar thought as he entered the house. After seeing the raw fear in his mother's eyes, he was beginning to understand what his father had meant.

"Anyu, what's wrong?" Oscar closed the door and faced his mother. Her usually rosy cheeks were drained of color.

Her hair, usually pulled back into a sleek bun, had come loose. Black strands curled around her face. She had dark smudges under her eyes from sleepless nights. The house was small. Sometimes, late at night when Paul was sound asleep, Oscar could hear her crying through the thin wall between their bedroom and hers.

"Anyu, what's wrong?" he repeated.

Paul tugged at Anyu's sleeve. "I want to go outside and play."

"No, Paul," she said. "You must stay in the house." She ushered the boys to the kitchen and told them to sit at the table.

Paul grabbed his usual chair, the one facing the sink. He squirmed. "I have to pee."

Their mother sighed. "Please, Oscar, take him outside. But come right back in."

Oscar grasped his brother's hand, and they went through the backdoor into the yard. He led Paul toward the mulberry tree, whose branches were furred from the first blossoms of spring. Beside it stood the wooden outhouse. Everything looked normal, yet Oscar knew that with the soldiers' arrival, nothing was the same. Even Paul, usually talkative, was quiet.

The boys went into the outhouse. The rusty hinges of the door squeaked as it opened. When they finished, they trudged, still silent, back to the house.

As they entered, there was a knock at the front door.

"Stay here," their mother ordered. She went to the door and opened it a crack. Aunt Bella, Anyu's best friend, squeezed into the room. The women fell into each other's arms.

"What is it?" Anyu asked.

"Mr. Gross wants everyone to come to the synagogue at seven o'clock." Since the rabbi's death four years earlier, Joseph Gross had assumed leadership of Karcag's Jewish community. "The Germans have issued orders," Bella continued. "He will tell us what we must do."

"Why are the Germans here, Auntie Bella?" asked Paul. Bella wasn't really his aunt, but Oscar and Paul had always called her that anyway.

The women eyed each other. "It'll be all right," said their mother. "We'll do what we must and everything will be well."

"But *why* are they here?" Paul asked again.

Aunt Bella knelt and met his eyes. "Why they are here isn't important. They are here! And we must do what they say to stay safe. Do you understand?" She stood, turning to leave. "I'll see you in the synagogue."

Anyu nodded. They returned to the kitchen, where Anyu ladled chicken soup into bowls from a big pot on the stove. She set them before Oscar and Paul with pieces of matzo.

"Eat."

She attempted a smile, but Oscar saw the strain on her face. He tried to smile back but couldn't. He turned to his soup, and they ate in silence.

Anyu looked at her watch. "It's almost seven. We must go to the synagogue."

Chapter 3

The synagogue was crowded when the family arrived. Anyu climbed the stairs to the balcony, to the women's section, while Oscar and Paul joined a group of boys on a bench at the back.

Paul looked around the familiar space. He loved this room, with its high ceilings, tall windows, and clean white walls. He had always felt comfortable here, but tonight things felt different. The old men who filled the seats were silent. Instead of shouting greetings to friends, they sat slumped in their seats. *Everyone is afraid,* Paul thought. *I wish Apu were here. He's strong. He would protect us.*

"Oscar." Paul grasped his brother's arm. "When is Apu coming home?"

Oscar felt a lump in his throat. Paul's face was hopeful and trusting, as if Oscar could ease his fears. What should he say?

"I don't know, Paul. No one knows."

"Will Mr. Gross tell us?"

"He doesn't know either."

"Are people scared of the soldiers?" Paul asked.

"Yes." Oscar swallowed. "They are frightening everyone. Maybe Mr. Gross can tell us what we're supposed to do. So sit still and listen."

Paul nodded and settled back in his seat.

Oscar turned to the front, where Mr. Gross was trying to quiet the crowd. "Please, everyone. We must remain calm. The German army has occupied Hungary and the Hungarian Gendarmes are in Karcag, carrying out their orders."

"Our own state police herding us like dogs!" shouted an old man from the first row. "Regent Horthy said that he would keep the German army out of Hungary!"

"And what does that matter now that Hungarians are the ones ordering us around?" said another man. "Besides, Horthy allied Hungary with the Germans. Who can trust him?"

"He claimed he did that so they wouldn't invade us," the first man replied. "I suppose it worked for four years."

"But now they're here, aren't they? Our regent made a deal with the Devil—that monster Hitler. Who expects the Devil to keep a promise?"

Paul listened to the angry voices. "Who is Horthy?" he whispered to Oscar.

"He's Hungary's regent. Our leader."

"Why is everyone mad at him?"

"I don't know, Paul. Stop pestering me with questions."

A man sitting in front of them turned around. "Boys, let me explain. When this war started, countries took sides. Hungary sided with Germany. For this, Germany said, 'Thank you. We will stay out of your country and leave you alone.' But now Germany has broken its promise."

"Is it Mr. Horthy's fault?" asked Oscar.

"No. He tried, but the Germans are bad people. They started the war and now everyone is suffering. Do you understand?"

"I think so," said Oscar.

Paul remained silent.

"Please, everyone, be quiet." Mr. Gross lifted his arms, signaling for silence. When that didn't work, he pounded on the lectern. "*Sha! Sha!* Arguing among ourselves won't solve anything." He held up a piece of paper. "The important thing now is to work together, follow orders, and not make trouble. The Germans have given us instructions." As the crowd settled down, he began to read.

"There is a curfew. Everyone must be off the streets by five o'clock." He paused and lowered his voice. "We are to sew yellow stars to our clothing and wear them whenever we leave our homes." His voice shook.

"The school is closed. Your businesses are closed. Everyone is to return home and await further instructions." He held his hands out, palms down, as if blessing the congregation.

"Have faith. God will protect us."

✡ ✡ ✡

"God will protect us! Like he protected my brother's family in Poland," a woman muttered, as they left the synagogue. "When the Germans entered Warsaw, my whole family disappeared. We haven't heard from them in over four years."

"*Sha.* Don't frighten the children." Anyu took Paul's hand and motioned for Oscar to follow. "We will do as the soldiers tell us and we will be well," she said as they walked home. She closed her eyes, and Paul saw tears run down her cheeks.

He'd never seen his mother cry. Suddenly, Paul was very afraid.

Chapter 4

The day after the soldiers arrived, the boys stayed home, since the school was closed. In the morning, their mother taught them their lessons. In the afternoon, they were allowed outside for an hour, to meet friends in the synagogue yard. Now they were sitting at the kitchen table. Oscar was working on arithmetic problems, and Paul, clutching a stubby pencil, was drawing on a piece of brown wrapping paper.

Paul looked up from his drawing at the window. He felt restless. He wanted to go outside and play with his friends, but Anyu said they had to stay in the house. He put down his pencil, slipped off the chair, and walked into the living room. His mother was in her rocking chair in the corner of the room, in front of the green tile stove that heated the house in winter.

"What is that, Anyu?" Paul asked, pointing to the star she was sewing onto his jacket.

"A decoration. Ouch!" Anyu cried as she pricked her finger with the needle. A drop of red blood spotted the star. She dropped the jacket and buried her face in her hands.

"Anyu, are you all right?" Paul touched his mother's cheek.

She looked up and gave him a weak smile, then sucked the wound. "See," she said, holding it out for his inspection, "it's nothing."

"Anyu, why do we have to wear the yellow stars?"

"Because the Germans say so," said Oscar. He emerged from the kitchen, his eyes glittering with anger.

"Will the gendarmes leave soon?" asked Paul. "I don't like them."

"Never say that in front of them," said Anyu. She pulled Paul onto her lap. "Promise me that you'll be a good boy and not cause any trouble."

"I promise, Anyu. But I still don't like them."

"I don't either." His mother gave him a sad smile.

For the next few weeks, life settled into a routine. Anyu continued to tutor the boys at home. Whenever they went out of the house, they were careful to wear their yellow stars. Spring was here and the trees filled with green leaves. When he was in the backyard, Paul watched birds build their nests. One day, he stepped outside and shouted.

"Anyu, Anyu! Come outside! Quick!"

Anyu hurried from the house, wiping her hands on her apron. There was a worried look on her face. "Paul, what is it? What's wrong?"

"Nothing's wrong, Anyu. Look." He pointed at the chimney. "The storks are back."

"Paul, you scared me to death." She sighed, but she didn't look angry. She placed an arm around Paul's shoulder. They both looked up at the chimney, where two storks were busy repairing a large nest of twigs and mud. Anyu waved at the birds.

"White storks bring luck. They leave Karcag every winter and return in the spring, to build nests and hatch their babies."

"I can't wait to see the babies." Paul jumped up and down, clapping his hands. It was nice to see his mother happy. "Thank you, stork," he mouthed. The bird stretched its long neck and made a clattering, *rat-a-tat-tat* sound.

"It's saying hello." Paul grinned.

"Yes, it is." Anyu bent down and kissed his cheek. "If the storks can come home, maybe Apu can, too."

✡ ✡ ✡

The storks' return brightened their spirits, but gendarmes still patrolled the streets, and everyone tried to stay out of their way. When they went to shop in the town square, Paul clung fearfully to his mother's hand.

"Anyu, why won't people look at us?" he asked.

They were standing in line at the bakery. The smell of fresh bread made his mouth water. The baker, a short, round man with twinkling blue eyes who usually gave him cookies, ignored them. When Anyu tried to get his attention, he looked away, as if she weren't there. The same thing happened at the green grocer, where Anyu went to buy onions and carrots.

His mother's shopping sack was only half full of the things she needed. It was getting harder and harder to get food. Paul had heard Anyu complain to Aunt Bella that soon they would be eating leaves off the trees.

"Why won't people look at us?" Paul repeated as they walked home.

"They think that if they are rude to us, the soldiers will treat them better."

"Will they?"

"Maybe, for a while. But the Nazis are bad people. They are cruel to everyone."

When they reached their house, Paul looked up at the chimney. The father stork was standing; the mother was sitting, keeping the eggs warm. "When will the babies hatch?" he asked.

"In about two weeks." As his mother gazed at the birds, her eyes misted. "It will be nice to have baby birds for houseguests."

"They look happy," said Paul. "I guess they don't know about the Germans."

"Yes, they are lucky." Anyu's voice cracked.

"We're lucky too, Anyu." Paul slipped his hand into hers. "Even if people like the baker are mean. Right, Oscar?" Paul squinted up at his brother who had just joined them.

"Sure, we're lucky. We have food and we're together."

"What about the soldiers?" Paul said.

"We have to do what they say and keep to ourselves so they will leave us alone." Oscar took Anyu's other hand. *At least for now*, he thought as they entered the house.

Chapter 5

On April 27, all the Jews of Karcag received the order that they were to be moved into an area at the edge of town. That night, after a supper of potato soup, Anyu told the boys that they would be leaving their house the following morning.

"Why?" asked Oscar.

"The Germans. They are creating a ghetto," Anyu muttered.

"What's a ghetto?" asked Paul.

"They want all the Jews of Karcag to live together on the same street. That's called a ghetto."

"I don't want to leave," said Paul.

Oscar just nodded. The cramped living room felt even smaller than usual. Everyone was quiet for a moment.

"Well," Anyu said, clearing her throat, "there is some good news. Auntie Bella and Kati and Magdi are going to be living with us. It could be fun."

Paul now brightened a bit. "We can play together all day."

"You will still have to do your lessons," Anyu reminded him.

"But we can play, too, can't we?"

Oscar glared at his brother. "Stop pestering Anyu."

"I'm not pestering her."

"You are, too."

"I am not." Paul stomped his foot.

"Boys, please." Anyu threw up her hands. "I have enough to worry about without you two fighting, too. Go to your room and get some sleep." Her face was white and her hands trembled. "Please, no more questions. Just do what I tell you."

✡ ✡ ✡

"Oscar, I'm scared," Paul said in bed later that night.

"There's nothing to be scared of." Oscar tried to steady his voice, but fear rippled across it.

"Anyu's scared, too," said Paul.

"No, she isn't."

"Yes, she is. I saw her cry while she was making supper."

"She's crying because she misses Apu. Now go to sleep. I don't want to have to pour water on your head to wake you in the morning."

For a minute, Paul was silent. Then he turned to face his brother. "Are the Germans bad people?"

"They're awful! I hate them! Them and the gendarmes they sent to watch us."

"Why?"

"Because they all hate us. They hate Jews."

"Why do they hate Jews? We haven't hurt them." Paul sat up and cupped his chin. "Maybe if we are nice to them, they'll be nice to us, too. Anyu said we should always treat people the way we want them to treat us."

Oscar sat on Paul's bed and put an arm across his shoulder. "Paul, that's true with most people, but we have to stay away from these soldiers."

"I don't understand."

"You don't have to understand. Just trust me and do what I say. Now be quiet and go to sleep."

"Good night, Oscar."

"Good night, Paul."

Paul turned on his side and was soon asleep, but Oscar lay awake, staring up at the ceiling and wondering what the next day would bring.

Chapter 6

"I still can't believe that they are making us live like this!" said Anyu.

She and Aunt Bella were sitting at the kitchen table of the tiny house where they had been forced to move three weeks ago. When they arrived along with the other Karcagi Jews, they found the area surrounded by a high barbed wire fence. Their house was a two-room home across the street from the cemetery.

"Beautiful, isn't it?" Bella grimaced as she looked around the room, before smiling gently. "Honestly, Anyu, some homes have four families inside. At least we are only two in here."

"For now," said Anyu. "The children want to know when they can go to school again. I told them that this situation was temporary, that soon life would be as it was before. But I don't believe it."

"Lenke, don't say that!" Aunt Bella leaned across the table and took Anyu's hand. "We will be all right as long as we stay together and do what they say. This war can't last forever. My cousin has a friend in Budapest who has a secret radio. He says that the British and the Americans are going to invade France soon. They will chase the Nazis back to Germany. We must stay hopeful."

Anyu sighed. "You believe that. Please, help me believe it, too." She stopped talking when Oscar and his friend Gabor entered the room.

"Anyu," said Oscar, "Gabor says the Germans are going to send us all away."

"Of course they will. That's what Germans do to Jews." Gabor sneered.

"You just want to frighten everyone." Oscar turned to his mother. "It's not true, is it, Anyu?"

"Stop it! Both of you." Anyu said.

"But is it true?" Oscar repeated. "Are they sending us away?"

"And where do you think they would send us? To Lake Balaton, for a vacation?" Aunt Bella's laugh came out as a bark.

She's scared, too, Oscar thought.

"The gendarmes gathered all the Jews in Szolnok last week and took them to the train station," said Gabor. "My cousin ran away. He's hiding in the Forgacses' barn. He says they are putting Jews in every town on trains."

Anyu waved a hand. "These are rumors. Please, boys, do not repeat them to the younger children."

Gabor raised his voice. "But he *saw* it…"

"Gabor!" Aunt Bella's voice cracked like a whip. "Don't speak of this again. Now you should go home. On your way out, please tell Paul and the girls to come in for lunch."

After the boys had left, the women exchanged terrified looks. "Lenke, it's true," Aunt Bella whispered. "Dearest God, I'm afraid the rumors are true."

"We can't let the children see us afraid," said Anyu. "Somehow, we must keep up our spirits."

She forced a smile as Paul, Oscar, and the girls came into the kitchen. Kati, with her dark hair and eyes, was a playful child who loved to tease Paul, a year younger. Magdi, the baby of the group, had just turned four and tagged after Paul and Kati like a puppy.

Paul came up to his mother. "Anyu, Oscar wouldn't let us play with him and Gabor."

"I said you could watch us play soccer," Oscar protested.

"I wanted to kick the ball."

"I'm a good soccer player," said Kati. She swung her leg high, pantomiming a kick.

"Me, too." Magdi imitated her sister.

"I told them that girls can't play with boys," Paul said. He turned to Oscar. "I tried to keep them out of your game."

"Anyu, Aunt Bella, please tell them to leave us alone," Oscar pleaded. "At least once in a while."

Anyu patted his shoulder. "Tomorrow I will organize a separate game for the little ones. You have been very patient."

"I don't want to be patient," Oscar muttered, as he stalked out of the room.

"It's hard for Oscar, being the oldest," said Aunt Bella.

"He's a good boy. He'll be all right." Anyu stood up from the table. "Let's have the children wash up for lunch."

"We're out of water," said Aunt Bella.

Anyu called into the next room. "Oscar, could you get us some water?"

"I want to go, too," Paul said.

Oscar came back into the kitchen. He grasped the metal pail by the handle with a sigh. "Let's go, Paul." The boys walked up the street to the water pump on the corner.

"Wait for me." Magdi trotted up behind them.

"Magdi, you shouldn't be out by yourself," said Oscar.

"I'm not by myself. I'm with you." Her eyes sparkled with mischief.

"I'll hold her hand," said Paul.

Oscar rolled his eyes. "All right. But let's hurry."

When they reached the water pump, Oscar handed Paul the pail. "You hold it while I pump."

Paul grasped the pail with both hands, careful to hold it directly below the spout.

"I want to help, too." Magdi grasped the bottom.

"Hold it steady." Oscar pushed the pump handle up and down. When the pail was full, he took it from Paul. It had rained earlier that day, and their shoes made splashing sounds as they tramped through the muddy puddles. No one was outside. The houses they passed had curtains drawn over closed windows. *It's as if everyone is hiding.* Oscar shivered and motioned for Paul and Magdi to walk faster.

"Thank you," said Aunt Bella as they came inside. "Now let's all wash our hands." She ladled the water into a ceramic bottle, which she held over a bowl. Oscar and the others gathered around her, hands outstretched as she poured the water over them. She handed them a bar of soap and then rinsed their hands. "Wipe them on the towel and then sit at the table," she said.

"Yes," said Anyu. "We don't want the soup to get cold. We—" She froze.

Someone was pounding on the front door.

Chapter 7

"Anyu?" asked Paul.

"Don't answer it."

The pounding grew louder. A voice barked, "Open up!"

Anyu wiped her hands on her apron. She walked into the living room, grasped the doorknob, and opened the door. Two soldiers pushed past her, almost knocking her down. Aunt Bella ran in, followed by Kati and Magdi.

"You, Jews! Outside! Now!"

Aunt Bella started to protest and the gendarme aimed his gun at her.

"Let's do what he says," Kati whispered. She took Magdi's hand. "Come outside."

Oscar took Paul's hand and walked out of the house with Anyu. The noon sun blinded him. He shielded his eyes with his hand as he took in the scene. Terrified people were spilling out of every doorway. Children clung to mothers as guards barked orders; old people stumbled as they were pushed into a line. The gendarmes had been joined by several German soldiers. Fear hit Oscar. *Why are they treating us this way?* He tightened his grip on Paul's hand, but Paul broke away.

"Avram!" Paul waved at a friend on the other side of the road. He started to cross over, but a German soldier with a giant dog blocked his way. The dog strained against its leash and thrust its face forward, level with Paul's. Drool dripped from its fangs as it growled; its eyes were a wicked yellow.

Paul shrank back toward Oscar, and the dog lunged. For a moment, he thought the animal would rip him apart. Then the soldier yanked the leash and moved down the line. Paul turned and buried his face in Oscar's shirt.

Oscar watched the soldier and fought back a wave of terror. He looked down at the yellow star on his shirt and then up at the guards herding them into a line.

They shouted orders for everyone to move forward. People shuffled along the dusty street, eyes cast down. As they were marched into the town square, Oscar remembered trips here, every Saturday after lunch. *This was where we met our friends. In the summer, we bought fresh fruit and vegetables from the farmers. And ice cream.* The thought made his mouth water.

"Look at *them*, watching us." Aunt Bella pointed to the townspeople gathered at the storefronts.

Oscar followed her gaze. Zoltan, the shoemaker, stood with his hands folded over his leather apron. Their eyes met and Zoltan looked away. Oscar recognized Tibor, a boy he had known all his life. A boy standing next to him shouted out, "Dirty Jews!"

Oscar expected Tibor to say something. They were good friends. Apu used to tutor him in math, and Anyu even taught him to play chess. *We used to play together, after school.*

"Dirty Jews!" The boy next to Tibor shouted again. This time Tibor echoed him.

Oscar turned away.

✡ ✡ ✡

The gendarmes made them stand in the square for hours. The day was hot; the sun beat down on their heads. As each hour passed, the younger children became more and more restless, but every time they started to move, a gendarme— or worse, a German soldier with a snarling dog—ordered them to be still. Paul shivered whenever he saw a dog. His legs ached from standing, and his mouth and throat were dry.

"Anyu, I'm so thirsty."

"Shh, Paul. We'll have water soon."

"When?"

"I don't know." She looked at the sky. The sun was getting low in the west. Soon it would be dark. At least it wouldn't be so hot. She wiped her forehead with her arm.

"No food, no water," Aunt Bella grumbled. "Not even for the children."

"What do they want from us?" asked Anyu.

The crowd of onlookers thickened. It seemed as if the whole town had come out to watch them. Finally, six canvas-topped trucks pulled into the square, and the gendarmes ordered them to climb in.

"Please, where are you taking us?" an elderly man asked one of the guards.

"None of your business," he snapped.

"My father is old and sick," begged the man's daughter. "I must go home for his medicine. I'll come right back."

"You'll go where you're told." The guard raised his gun.

The woman moved back into line, supporting her father as he stumbled.

Oscar helped his mother and brother climb over the tailgate into the truck. Once inside, they were pushed to the front as more and more people piled in, until it became so crowded there was no room to sit. The gendarmes shut the door, and Oscar braced his legs as the truck lurched forward.

Paul was crushed in a sea of legs. There wasn't room to sit, so he leaned against his mother's legs as the truck bounced and swayed over dirt roads. He didn't understand what was happening. *Where were they taking them?*

He looked up at his mother. She was staring straight ahead, one hand on his head, the other around Oscar's shoulders. Kati was clutching Aunt Bella's hand; Magdi the other. No one in the truck spoke. It was if their voices had been sucked out of them.

He closed his eyes. Maybe this was a bad dream, and he would wake up and they would all be safe at home.

Chapter 8

Szolnok, Hungary
June 1944

An hour later, the truck stopped and the gendarmes ordered them to get out. Paul looked up at Oscar, who gave him an encouraging smile. They moved to the back of the truck. Oscar climbed down and then helped his mother and brother. They were in front of a barbed-wire fence with a sign that read, "Szolnok Sugar Factory."

The gendarmes herded them through a gate into a large open yard, where a windowless building sat next to railroad tracks. An engine in front of a string of boxcars puffed out clouds of black smoke. More trucks pulled up outside the fence and soon the yard was full of tired, frightened people.

Oscar led his mother and brother to an empty spot by the fence. Aunt Bella and the girls followed. They sat on the ground and settled down to wait.

What are we waiting for? What are they going to do to us? Oscar put his head in his hands, covering his ears to blot out the noise: babies crying, women wailing, dogs barking. He looked up at the train. The boxcars' doors were open, forming a string of dark caverns. *Are we the cargo?* His stomach knotted. He felt like throwing up.

"Oscar." Paul tugged at his sleeve. "I need a toilet."

Oscar looked at his mother. "I'll take him, Anyu."

"Thank you." She gave him a tired smile.

The boys threaded their way through the crowded yard. A guard stopped them and then pointed to a spot against a brick wall where several other boys were relieving themselves. Some were standing; others squatting. One boy stuck out his tongue.

"Just ignore them," Oscar told Paul.

When they were finished, they rejoined their mother.

Oscar looked through the fence. An old woman pushed a cart filled with freshly baked bread. The delicious aroma made his mouth water. Behind her, a boy led a mooing cow. A young girl passed by, a water bucket in each hand. *Why are they so unconcerned? Don't they know what's happening to us?* He thought of Tibor, pretending not to see him and then calling him a "dirty Jew." *How could a person change so fast?*

Aunt Bella followed Oscar's gaze. "What are you thinking?"

"They are scared to look at us. They are afraid of the soldiers," said Oscar. "I hate them." He spat out the words. "I hate them all."

A blast of the train's whistle brought them to attention. The gendarmes started rounding up people and pushing them toward the boxcars.

"Stay still," their mother instructed. "Don't make them notice us."

"Where are they taking us?" asked a woman nearby.

"Maybe they will take us to Budapest," answered a second woman in a shaky voice.

"No. They are taking us east," answered a man.

"Don't say that," snapped the first woman.

"Why does going east frighten everyone?" Oscar asked her.

"Because that's where the concentration camps are—no one ever comes back from those camps."

"What kind of camps?" Oscar turned to his mother.

"Camps where they kill people," shouted the second woman. "In Poland, Jews are dying in a camp they call Auschwitz. I heard about it on the British radio station. Two men escaped, and they are telling the world what's happening. Only the world doesn't want to know."

"Stop it!" Anyu shook a finger in the woman's face. "Don't scare the children."

"Those stories are just propaganda. They tell them to frighten us," said Aunt Bella. "You are helping the enemy by spreading such rumors."

"I only hope you don't find out for yourselves." The woman wiped her eyes with her sleeve. "God forbid that we should end up in such a place."

"Enough!" Anyu stepped between Aunt Bella and the woman. "Such talk only frightens everyone and does no good. Oscar, don't listen to their gossip." She looked around in sudden panic. "Where's Paul? My God, they'll take him away!"

"I'll get him, Anyu," Oscar said quickly.

He was happy to get away from that woman and her gloomy talk. *I won't believe it,* he thought as he pushed his way through the crowd. *I can't believe it.*

Oscar finally found his brother playing on the far side of the yard with a group of boys. They had gathered pebbles for a game. A boy flicked one, and the next tried to hit it with his.

"Look, Oscar." Paul pointed proudly to his pile of pebbles. "I'm winning."

Oscar breathed a sigh of relief. "Come on, we've got to go back."

"But, Oscar, I want to play some more."

"No. We have to stay together. I don't want you to get lost."

Paul pushed his pile of stones to another boy. "Here, you can have these now."

He took Oscar's hand.

Oscar glanced at a guard standing nearby. He wore a gendarme's uniform, so Oscar knew he was Hungarian. He seemed younger than the others, with sandy hair and fair skin. He looked uneasy as he watched them. It seemed to Oscar that he wore his uniform like a costume—something he would take off when he finished playing the part, to go back to being the person he really was.

As Oscar stared up at him, the man returned his gaze. His eyes met Oscar's, and his expression softened. *He almost looks nice.* Oscar could feel some of his hatred leaving. Then an officer walked up and barked something in German. The gendarme snapped to attention, saluted, and clicked his heels. As he did so, he shot Oscar a warning look. Oscar shivered. The officer had double lightning bolts pinned to his lapel. From the day they had marched into Karcag, Oscar had learned the difference between regular German soldiers and those were part of the dreaded *Schutzstaffel*, the SS. They were the cruelest of all—the gendarme seemed as afraid of him as Oscar was.

Wheew-eee! Oscar jumped at the blast of the train whistle. Suddenly, the gendarmes were shouting, gesturing at people to go to the train. A woman, calling for her son, ran the other way. A gendarme ordered her to stop and when she refused, he cracked his whip across her face. The woman screamed. He grabbed her shoulder, turned her around, and pushed her onto the train.

"Don't look." Oscar pulled Paul close. He felt like he was caught in a strong wind shoving them toward the train. "Paul, hold on to me. We've got to get back to Anyu."

He pulled Paul along as he worked his way through the swirling crowd. Somehow they made it without getting caught.

"Anyu." Paul ran into his mother's arms.

"Thank God." Anyu pulled them both close. "Don't leave my sight again. We must stay together. Do you understand?" She looked sternly at Paul.

"Yes, Anyu." He lowered his eyes. "I promise."

Anyu turned to Aunt Bella. "Where are the girls?"

"We're here, Auntie Lenke," said Kati.

Magdi peeked out from behind her mother's skirt, where she'd been hiding.

The train whistle blew again. Everyone turned to watch as the gendarmes slid the door to the last boxcar shut.

"We are spared," Bella said.

"For today." Anyu watched the train leave the station. "At least for today."

Chapter 9

They had been in the yard by the factory for three days. Paul was tired, hungry, and filthy. He couldn't remember ever feeling good. He was so hungry his stomach cramped. All they'd eaten was some stale bread the gendarmes gave them.

He stood and looked around. People were scattered throughout the once-crowded station. Trains had been leaving every day. When would it be their turn? Where would they go? He crawled into his mother's lap.

"I'm hungry."

"My poor baby." She wrapped him in her arms.

Oscar took Paul's hand. "Let's get some water."

"I'll go with you," Kati said.

"I want to come, too." Magdi jumped to her feet. She looked up at Oscar with eyes dulled by hunger. "Please, can I come?"

"We're only going to the water fountain, not to the swimming pool at the Berek," Kati said.

"But it's something to *do*," Magdi whined. "I want to do *something*."

"All right, you can come," Kati said. She held out her hand. "Where do you think they're going to take us?" she asked Oscar as they crossed the yard.

"I don't know." Oscar frowned. "But I'm worried."

They reached the water spigot, which was on the other side of the windowless building. The water dripping from it was brown with rust. "The water we got at our well tasted better," Paul said, as he bent down and cupped his hands to catch a few drops.

"At least it was clean," said Oscar. He watched as Kati drank, and then he bent down and opened his mouth under the spigot. He grimaced. The rusty water tasted metallic like blood. He finished and looked up as a train whistle blew. The whistle hooted again as the train squealed to a stop.

"We'd better go back." Oscar grabbed Paul, and Kati took Magdi's hand. As they started across the yard, a gendarme blocked their path.

"Where do you think you're going?" He grabbed Kati's shoulder. "Get on the train."

"We need to go to our mothers," Kati said.

A German soldier, who was fighting to restrain his dog, stepped forward and shoved her roughly.

"You'll go where we tell you," the gendarme said.

The dog growled.

Aunt Bella ran up to them. "All of you come with me." She looked up at the gendarme. "We are together."

The dog was still barking, and the soldier bent to adjust its leash.

"Come!" Aunt Bella pulled them over to Anyu, who was waving frantically. "It's all right, Lenke. We are all here now."

The yard was a scene of chaos. Dogs barked, guards shouted, and people gathered their children and bundles as the gendarmes herded everyone toward the train. Some of the older people were too weak to walk and had to be supported by others. When an old man fell, a guard kicked him until he struggled to his feet. A little girl was crying for her mother. A guard picked her up and threw her into the boxcar.

Oscar grasped Paul's hand. "Hold on to me. Don't let go," he commanded.

"Yes, Oscar." Paul clutched so tightly his fingernails dug into Oscar's skin.

"Move!" A guard prodded them with the butt of his gun. Oscar saw that it was the same gendarme who had looked at them kindly the other day. He searched his face for some recognition, but any hint of compassion had disappeared. The gendarme showed only anger as he waved his gun. Oscar's knees buckled and he grabbed his mother for support.

They reached the boxcar. Paul peered through the dark opening. "I don't want to go in there," he said.

"I'll go first." Oscar climbed up and then helped his mother and brother into the car. Aunt Bella and the girls followed. People piled in until there was no room to sit. When the car was full, the door slammed shut and everything went black.

✡ ✡ ✡

It took a few minutes for Oscar's eyes to adjust to the darkness. Slivers of light leaked through slits in the boxcar's walls. By squinting, he was able to make out shapes of people huddled together. Beside him Paul whimpered. Oscar put an arm around him.

"Don't be afraid, little brother. I'll take care of you."

"I want to go home." Paul's voice trembled.

"Soon, but now we're on a train. Imagine that! We've never been on a train before. This is an adventure."

"I don't like this adventure."

"Oscar…" Anyu's voice was tired. "Don't tease him."

"I'm not teasing him, Anyu. I'm telling him not to be scared."

"I'm scared, too," Magdi piped up.

"Listen to Oscar," said Kati. "This is exciting. We are going to see new places."

"Really?" said Paul. "What kind of places?"

"Oh, I don't know." Oscar lowered his voice. "Magic places with lakes and trees, maybe even a mountain."

"I've never seen a mountain," said Magdi.

"Me neither," said Paul. He yawned. "I'm sleepy." He leaned against Oscar, rested his head against him, and promptly fell asleep.

"We should all try to sleep," Aunt Bella said.

"Or at least rest," Anyu said. "We can lean against each other for support."

Around them people were quieting down—whether from terror, exhaustion, or resignation, Oscar couldn't tell. He closed his eyes and prayed that at least some of the story he had told Paul, Kati, and Magdi would be true.

Chapter 10

Vienna, Austria
June 1944

"The train has stopped!"

Paul opened his eyes. The air in the car was sour with the smell of unwashed bodies and an overflowing slop bucket. Around him people were stirring. A baby cried; a woman moaned. In the corner of the car an old man wailed. Someone told him to be quiet. The door of the car slid open, and Paul blinked in the sudden light.

"Out! Everyone out!" a soldier ordered.

Paul struggled to move. His legs were stiff from standing for many hours in a tight space. Oscar took his hand to steady him. They made their way to the front of the car. People ahead of them climbed down onto the platform. When it was their turn, Oscar went down first and then helped Paul and Anyu.

"Where are we?" Paul asked.

"Vienna." Aunt Bella pointed to a sign hanging over the platform. She turned to Anyu. "Why did they bring us here?"

Anyu shrugged. She looked along the train. People were pouring out of every car, filling the platform. Soldiers were ordering them onto a second train stopped on the other side. These were no longer the Hungarian Gendarmerie. All of them were German, with the SS insignia on their collars.

There were people everywhere. She reached out for Paul, but he wasn't there.

"Oscar, where's Paul?"

"I don't know, Anyu. He was with you."

"Paul. Paul!" she called. She searched the crowd but didn't see him. "He's so small…"

A guard pushed them forward. "You! Into that car, over there."

"I have to find my son. He's missing."

"You should have taken better care of him." The guard sneered. "Now get on that train before I shoot you and your other boy." He pointed the gun at Oscar.

"Lenke," Aunt Bella said, "we'll find Paul when we get off."

"I have to find him now!" Anyu sobbed.

"Anyu, *please!*" Oscar looked fearfully at the guard fingering the trigger of his gun.

Aunt Bella and the girls were already being forced up into in the boxcar. Oscar was tugging at Anyu's arm. She took one last frantic look around the station.

No Paul.

Clutching her chest, as if trying to hold her breaking heart together, she took Oscar's hand and they climbed into the car. Crushed among a mass of people, Anyu watched the door slide shut. As the last of the daylight faded, so did her hopes of finding her son.

✡ ✡ ✡

Paul stood on the platform and looked for someone, anyone familiar.

Where was Anyu? What had happened to Oscar?

He couldn't find Aunt Bella or the girls. People were pressing in on him, knocking him from one side to another. He looked up. Everyone was so big. He was lost in a tangle of arms and legs.

"Anyu!" he screamed, but no one answered. *Where are they? I want my mother. I want my brother.* He burst into tears.

"Are you lost, little boy?"

Paul looked up at a Nazi guard. He didn't understand the man's words, but he recognized the cruel look in his icy blue eyes. He was tugging at the leash of an enormous dog. The dog bared its teeth and drool leaked from its mouth. Paul trembled. He was so scared that he was afraid he would pee his pants.

The soldier leaned down and pushed his face against Paul's. "We can't leave you alone here on the platform, can we?" He grabbed him under his arms and hoisted him to the mouth of a railroad car.

Paul fell forward. He tried to stand up, but there wasn't any room. The door slammed shut and the car went dark. He groped about, looking for a place to sit, and, finding none, squeezed in between two women who be grudgingly made space for him. The boxcar was so crowded he couldn't breathe. He pulled his knees to his chest, lowered his head, and cried until he fell asleep.

Chapter 11

The minute they got off the train, Oscar and his mother started searching for Paul. Oscar ran in one direction while she went the other way.

As each boxcar emptied, Oscar called his brother's name and asked people if they had seen him. Forcing his way through the crowd, he looked at every young boy, but none of them was Paul.

The guards were shoving people into a line. Oscar was afraid that he would become separated from Anyu, too, but he had to find Paul.

And then he saw a dark, curly head bobbing through the crowd.

"Paul!" he shouted.

"Oscar!" Paul zigzagged along the platform, wiggling his way between legs. He jumped into his brother's outstretched arms and burrowed against his shoulder. Inside he was still shaking, but he pretended he wasn't scared.

"I was brave," Paul said, as they made their way back to Anyu.

"Sure you were." Oscar tousled his hair. "But stay with us from now on. Don't worry Anyu." *Or me*, he thought.

Anyu hugged Paul and covered his face with kisses.

"Oh, my little Pauli, don't scare us like that again. You promise?"

"I promise," Paul said solemnly. "Anyu, I was brave." He buried his face in her skirt as he fought back tears.

"You, over there!" A soldier motioned with his gun for the family to join the line they were forming.

"There are Bella and the girls." Anyu pointed. "Come." She led her children to the place in line where they were standing.

Aunt Bella hugged her. "I was afraid something had happened to all of you."

"I got lost," Paul said. "Oscar found me."

"He was in a different car." Anyu's voice trembled.

"Stop worrying your mother!" Aunt Bella shook a finger in Paul's face. "Do you hear me?"

"Yes, Auntie Bella. Where are we going?"

"I don't know," she said, as the line began to move. "Just stay together, everyone. And pray," she added under her breath, "pray hard."

Chapter 12

Strasshof Concentration Camp, Austria
July 1944

"Where are we now?" asked Kati.

"Somewhere in Austria." Oscar pointed to a sign by the station house.

"Austria. Thank God." Anyu sighed. "At least we're not in Germany."

"Or, God forbid, Poland," Aunt Bella added. The women exchanged knowing looks.

"What's wrong with Poland?" asked Kati.

Aunt Bella just shook her head.

Oscar thought of the conversation in the brickyard about the Polish concentration camp. *At least we're not there.* He took a deep breath. Wherever they were going had to be better than Auschwitz.

"Go!" Aunt Bella nudged her daughter as the guards ordered them into a truck.

"They never tell us anything," Kati whispered to Oscar. "We're old enough to know what's going on."

"They don't want to scare us," Oscar replied.

"Don't want to scare us? How much more scared could we be?" Kati pointed to Magdi, pale as snow. "She hasn't said a word for hours."

Ahead of them a small girl cried out and a soldier turned his gun on her. Her mother screamed and covered the child's body with her own. For a moment the woman and the soldier stared at each other. Then he pushed them toward the truck.

Paul climbed into the truck. His legs were trembling. He looked at his mother whose eyes were black against her pale, pinched face. He reached up and touched her cheek. "I won't get lost again, Anyu. I promise."

"I won't let you." She kissed the top of his head. She pulled Oscar to her. "You will watch over your brother."

"I will, Anyu." Oscar puffed out his chest. "I'm the man in the family. Apu said so."

"Yes." Anyu sighed. Her eyes had a faraway look. She placed her hand under Oscar's chin. "My strong young man."

Paul cuddled close to his mother. He rubbed his face against her dress and wrapped his arms around her waist. For the rest of the ride he held on tight, as if afraid letting go would make her disappear.

After a short ride the truck stopped. Soldiers lowered the tailgate and ordered everyone out. They lined up in front of a table where a guard entered their names on a list. A row of guards with dogs stood behind them.

Paul shivered. The soldiers were frightening, but their dogs scared him the most. They were huge. And they had sharp teeth and angry eyes.

After the soldiers recorded their names, they were taken to an open area where soldiers were spraying people with giant hoses. The guards ordered them to take off their clothes.

"Not in front of our children!" Aunt Bella begged the soldier.

In answer, he rattled the chain of the German shepherd at his side. The dog growled and lunged forward. The guard pulled him back and then pointed toward the soldiers hosing down a group of nude women.

"You go there," he said.

Aunt Bella sighed. "Lenke, Kati, Magdi, let's go." They walked over to the shower area and got in line.

Oscar covered his brother's eyes as Anyu, Aunt Bella, and the girls were forced to strip. Paul peered over his brother's hand, but Oscar turned him around. He didn't want Paul to see their mother struggling to cover her body with her hands.

When it was their turn, the boys took off their clothes and waited in front of the soldiers holding the hose.

"Hold on to me," Oscar said, as the water hit them.

Before Paul could grab Oscar's hand, he was hit with a blast of frigid water. The harsh spray stung his face, especially his eyes, and icy needles rained down his body. He turned and the water struck his back, almost knocking him down.

"Get dressed," the soldiers ordered when it was over. Oscar helped Paul into his shirt and shorts and then dressed himself. The clothes stuck to their wet skin.

"At least we're clean," Oscar quipped.

The soldiers lined them up and marched them into a long, low building, where they were assigned bunk beds, three people to each level. Exhausted, they lay down, Paul on the inside, Oscar in the middle, and Anyu on the outside. The bunk was narrow and hard. Bella and the girls took a bunk across the aisle.

Oscar turned onto his side, trying to get comfortable.

"Oscar, I'm scared." Paul whimpered

"Don't be frightened, Paul. Go to sleep. Everything will be better tomorrow."

"Good night, Oscar. Good night, Anyu." Paul was too exhausted to think. He closed his eyes and allowed himself to disappear into sleep.

The two families stayed in the Strasshof Concentration Camp for two weeks. During that time they lived in the barracks and were fed watery soup and stale bread once a day. They soon realized that this was a holding camp, where people were kept until going to their final destination. Every day, new people arrived in Strasshof and others were taken away.

Anyu and Aunt Bella worried constantly about where they would be sent. Then one day, two weeks after they'd arrived, the families were loaded onto trucks and driven away from the camp.

Chapter 13

Guntersdorf, Austria
July 1944

The family stood inside a long wooden building. Piles of straw dotted the dirt floor.

"Are those our beds?" Paul asked.

"Yes, darling." Anyu smiled. "At least this isn't a concentration camp."

"This is a barn. I can smell the cows," Paul grinned. It was good to see his mother smiling. She looked almost happy. "I like it here," he told Oscar.

"We're on a farm," his brother replied. "Maybe here we'll have enough to eat."

✡ ✡ ✡

That morning, when they had been loaded into one of three trucks, Paul had been scared. He had thought of his terrifying time being lost and had clung to his mother and brother. As they drove into the hills, Paul sat near the tailgate and peered through the slats. The road twisted through fields where farmers were tending their crops. He saw cows grazing on new grass.

Paul turned to Oscar. "It's pretty here."

"Yes, it is. It looks like the farmland around Karcag." Oscar stood and looked over the railing.

The truck passed a horse cart filled with bags of what looked like potatoes. The man driving it averted his eyes as the truck passed. *Just like the people in Karcag,* Oscar thought. *He doesn't want to see us.*

After an hour, the truck turned onto a dirt road and stopped. Again, they were ordered off by soldiers and put into lines. Paul forced himself to stand motionless as a soldier marched up and down the line, checking their names against a list on his clipboard. When everyone was accounted for, the soldier divided them into four groups, and then other soldiers marched each group into a barn-like structure. The inside had been emptied except for straw mattresses on the floor. Each mattress had a blanket.

"Good, I don't have to sleep with Oscar, like in the last camp," Paul said as he plopped down on a mattress.

"Yeah, I'll miss your foot in my mouth." Oscar studied their mother as she sank onto an adjoining mattress. Her glossy black hair had faded. Her eyes were dull and her shoulders sagged. Ever since the icy shower she had been coughing. He hoped rest and fresh air would make her better. He looked at his brother. Paul had regained some of his energy and was bouncing on the mattress. For once, Anyu didn't scold him. She seemed too tired to react. At that moment two of the farmer's workers came in with food. They gave everyone a metal bowl and a spoon. Then they ladled soup into the bowl and handed each person a slice of bread.

People sat on their mattresses eating. When they were done, they were told to keep their utensils for the rest of their meals.

"Come on. Let's go outside and wash the dishes." Oscar led Paul and the girls out of the barn. Their feet raised dust whorls as they crossed the yard. Paul sneezed and a chicken squawked and fluttered out of their way.

Paul stopped. "Oscar, what are those?"

Oscar looked where Paul was pointing. "Whew," he whistled. "Mountains."

"Like you said on the train?" said Kati.

"Yes, just like that." Oscar had never seen mountains before either, but he knew what they looked like from pictures in a book at school.

"Why are they white?" asked Magdi.

"They're covered in snow." Although it was June, the peaks were capped with a frosty mantle. As they watched, the snow turned rosy from the setting sun. "It's getting late. Let's wash the dishes and go back inside."

"Oscar," Paul said as they crossed the yard, "what are we going to do tomorrow?"

"I don't know."

"Do you think we can go to the mountains?"

"No. We'll have to do what the soldiers tell us." Oscar stopped and looked down at his brother. "Promise me you'll be good and do what you're told."

"Yes, Oscar," Paul said seriously. "I promise." He took his brother's hand. Magdi grabbed his other hand and they all walked back to the barn.

✡ ✡ ✡

The guards woke them at dawn and ordered everyone to line up outside. In the early morning chill, Paul shivered as he stood between his mother and brother as an armed guard walked slowly up the line and another called out names.

"*Stand still,*" Oscar hissed in Paul's ear when he started to move.

Paul held his breath as the guard stopped in front of them.

"*Keep still,*" Oscar whispered as the guard moved past them.

He would soon learn that these lineups, or *appels* as the Germans called them, were the most difficult part of their daily routine. And he learned to look for the SS pins on soldiers' collars, because those soldiers were the ones to be feared the most.

After what seemed like forever, the guard blew his whistle and everyone returned to their barn. Aunt Bella walked over as Anyu collapsed onto her mattress.

"Lenke, how do you feel?" Aunt Bella bent down and placed a hand on her friend's forehead.

"I will live." Anyu gave her a weak smile. "Look, they are bringing us food."

Everyone took out their dishes as two farm workers handed out breakfast—a piece of bread and coffee. After eating, a guard ordered them to go back outside. This time, the farm owner greeted them. The guards stood in front of him, guns at their sides. Other guards patrolled the line with their dogs.

"*Guten morgen,*" the farmer stammered. He looked uncomfortable as he surveyed the assembled prisoners. He was tall with muscled arms. He had a farmer's leathery skin, from being outdoors so much.

He doesn't look mean, Oscar thought. The farmer's wife stood beside him. She was a stout woman with blond hair, blue eyes, and a kindly face. Like her husband, she seemed uncomfortable giving orders.

The farmer cleared his throat. "You have been brought here to Austria to help us bring in a good harvest. For the Fatherland," he added, with a sideways glance at the Nazi guards. "This farm grows sugar beets. You will work in groups…"

The farmer spoke German and one of the prisoners, a young woman who had taught German in a high school, translated his words into Hungarian. His voice droned on and Oscar used the time to look around. They were standing in front of a vast field. In the distance, he saw the mountains, now purple in the morning haze.

When the farmer finished, he stepped aside and a guard replaced him. As always, a dog hunched beside him.

"You are prisoners of the Third Reich and will do what you are told. Follow orders and there will be no trouble." He fixed them with a steely gaze. "Am I understood?"

Oscar nodded. He looked at Paul and saw that he was nodding, too. Good. Oscar knew that his biggest challenge would be keeping Paul in line. He looked at his mother, who seemed to have gained strength since breakfast. *Maybe this won't be so bad,* he thought. *It's getting warmer and we're on a farm. Farms mean food. Maybe the war will end soon and we can go home.*

Yet, when he looked at the German soldiers, so strong and unbeatable, he doubted that his life would ever return to what it was like before the war.

Chapter 14

The work on the farm was hard but not unbearable. Paul and the other young children were given jobs carrying water to the laborers who tended the sugar beet plants. Oscar and other children his age worked beside the adults. The days were warm, so their thin clothes were sufficient. Their mother washed them once a week, wrapping the boys in blankets while the clothes dried on a line outside the barn. Every night, she used her comb to check their hair for lice and made them clean their teeth with pieces of straw.

Paul made friends among the other boys and girls. When the workday was over, he'd play with them while Oscar hung out with the older children. They tried to pretend they were in a summer camp, not a German labor camp. Yet the truth crept in: when they had to line up and the soldiers patrolled them with their guns and snarling dogs, or when they worked long hours under the stern gaze of the soldiers, or, worst of all, when someone became ill and was taken away—and never seen again.

When they weren't working, the children played skipping games or hide-and-seek, while their mothers sat and talked.

"Anyu, where is Apu?" Paul asked one day.

He was sitting outside with his mother and two other women. They had finished their supper of boiled potatoes, beets, and bread and were resting. It was early August, so it was still light at seven o'clock. Paul closed his eyes. The jangle of cowbells, the smell of freshly mown hay, and the taste of the raspberries the children had picked from nearby bushes reminded him of home.

"I wish Apu were here with us." He gave his mother a wistful look.

"I do, too, Paul." Anyu stroked his head. "I wish I knew where he was and that he was safe."

"Maybe we're better off not knowing where our men are," said Eva, a woman from their barrack.

"*Sha*, don't say that." Anyu covered Paul's ears.

"I know that my grandparents are dead," Eva moaned.

"Are my grandparents dead, too?" Paul asked.

"You shouldn't think about such things." Anyu turned to the other women. "This is not a conversation we should have around our children. Paul, I would love some more berries." She handed him her dish. "Please pick some for me."

"Yes, Anyu." He took the dish and walked to the side of the barn where the raspberry bushes grew. As he rounded the corner, he heard the women's voices talk more.

"Our husbands, parents—they could all be dead," Eva said.

Paul bent down and concentrated on picking as many berries as he could stuff in his mouth, then he filled his dish. It was getting dark. An owl hooted in the distance.

"Paul," his mother called. "Paul, we are going inside."

Paul walked back to the barrack. As he approached, the women stopped talking.

Chapter 15

In September, after they had been on the farm for almost three months, the work got harder. The sugar beets were ready for harvesting and everyone worked the fields to dig them up before the first frost. Paul was still a water boy, a job he enjoyed because he could move freely up and down the rows of sugar beets. Oscar was one of the harvesters, working alongside the adult women. He was working his row of beets when Paul came running up to him.

"Oscar, Auntie Bella wants you."

Oscar gently pulled a sugar beet plant from the ground and put it into his basket. He looked around to make sure none of the guards were watching and then hurried over to Aunt Bella.

"What's wrong?"

"Your mother." She pointed to Anyu, sitting on the ground, her head in her hands.

"Anyu!" Oscar bent down. "Are you sick?"

"I'm all right," his mother said. "It's just the sun. It made me dizzy."

Oscar looked up. He couldn't see the sun. The sky was heavy with rain-swollen clouds. "Is this the first time this has happened?" Oscar asked Aunt Bella.

"No." She shook her head. "She didn't want you or Paul to know, but she has been ill for several weeks now." Aunt Bella looked over her shoulder. "She has to pick her quota of beets or the Germans..." She let the sentence hang in the air.

Oscar knelt down. For the last few weeks he'd been worried about his mother. She was losing weight and getting weaker every day. Now, he was terrified. If she was sick, she might be sent away. He couldn't let that happen.

"Don't worry, Anyu. I'll pick the beets for you."

"No, I can do it." His mother struggled to her feet. She bent over, reached for a plant, and collapsed. "Just another minute," she said, shielding her eyes with her hand.

"Anyu, are you sick?" Paul appeared, holding a water bucket. He gave his mother a drink and then offered water to the others.

Anyu smiled up at him. "My little water boy."

"Yes. I give everyone water. It's a very important job." Paul grinned, exposing a gap where he had just lost his first tooth.

"Go." Oscar shooed him away. "Bring water to the others."

Paul trotted off. Oscar reached down and plucked the sugar beet his mother had been trying to pull out of the ground. He put it into her basket and moved down the row, gathering beets as he went. When he had finished his mother's row, he went back to his own and finished that in double time. He couldn't let the guards realize she was sick.

He stood, stretched, and rubbed the back of his neck. Picking the beets was hard work, even for him. It meant bending over for hours at a time. His back hurt, but he was young and strong. Paul was all right because he was a water boy and thought of this as a game.

When their shift was over, everyone lined up in front of their barn. It was time for roll call. Every day, morning and evening, the German guards counted them. Sometimes they would stand in line for hours. Oscar remembered Anyu shivering as sheets of water drenched them for almost a whole day last week. The guards had laughed. Another woman had started coughing. When she couldn't stop, a guard grabbed her by the hair, pulled her out of line, and threw her to the ground. The woman's coughing stopped. As she crawled back into the lineup, the guard kicked her so she fell forward into the mud face-first.

Oscar vowed he would never let something like that happen to Anyu.

✡ ✡ ✡

"Rest, Lenke, rest."

Oscar watched as Aunt Bella placed a wet cloth on Anyu's forehead.

They were back in the barn and Anyu was lying on her bed. Oscar stood beside her. "Anyu, are you sick?"

"No, darling." She took his hand. "I'm not sick, I'm tired." She turned to Bella. "And worried. Bella, where are the men? What has happened to our parents, to our sisters, and brothers, and their children? What is this madness doing to our families?"

Oscar swallowed. He was worried, too. And scared. *What if we never see Apu again?*

"Anyu, please don't worry." He gave her a shaky smile. "The workers just brought supper. I'll get you some food. You'll feel better after you eat."

Anyu squeezed his hand. "When did you become the man of the family?"

As he walked away, Oscar heard his mother say, "The harvest is almost finished. Do you know where we will go next?"

He didn't hear Aunt Bella's answer. He wasn't sure that he wanted to know.

He walked outside. His brother was playing tag with Kati and Madgi and some other children. *I wish I could be like them*, Oscar thought. But he was frightened. Whenever the SS officers wanted to scare someone, they threatened to send them east. And he remembered the conversation in the brickyard, when the women were discussing Auschwitz. The thought of going to such an awful place terrified him. He had heard that the conditions were dreadful. People became ill. They were killed or died of disease. He had promised Apu that he would protect his mother and brother. *I will try to keep my promise.*

But what if I can't? It was a possibility that Oscar didn't even want to consider.

Chapter 16

"Wake up, birthday boy. It's October 30, and you are six years old!

Paul opened his eyes. His mother was smiling. She bent down and kissed him. Paul threw his arms around her neck. "I'm six years old!" He jumped up from his mattress.

"Hey, brat, stop making so much noise." Oscar turned away from him, eyes still shut.

"But it's my birthday. Anyu, can I have a cake?"

For a moment, his mother looked sad. Then she brightened. "Not a cake, but we will do something special. Tonight."

✡ ✡ ✡

That evening, after they had eaten, everyone in their barn gathered around Paul to wish him a happy birthday. One woman brought out some apricots she had secretly gathered from trees on the farm and dried over the summer.

"A birthday treat," he said, as she passed them around.

"Happy birthday, Paul." Kati hugged him.

"I'm going to be five soon," said Magdi. She handed him a small stone. "I found it. See," she said, pointing, "it's shaped like a frog."

"Thank you, Magdi." Paul pecked her cheek.

"What's all this noise?" A guard appeared in the doorway. "You should all be in bed." He turned off the lights and shut the door.

Everyone went to their beds.

"It was a nice birthday," Paul said as he settled down. And clutching his frog-shaped rock, he fell asleep.

Chapter 17

"Up! Out! Everyone!"

Oscar awoke with a start. Soldiers were tramping through the barn, ordering everyone outside. He staggered to his feet and looked over to his mother, sitting on the edge of her bed. Paul began to scamper for the doorway.

"Paul, wait for me," Oscar ordered. "Anyu, here, take my hand." He helped his mother up and held her arm.

"Move! Outside!" the soldier barked.

"Paul, take Anyu's other hand."

"I can walk." His mother said, moving forward.

"Oscar, is Anyu all right?" Paul looked from his mother to his brother.

"She's very tired."

Paul didn't think his mother was just tired. Every day she became weaker and weaker and it frightened him. They walked outside and joined the line of prisoners. Paul shivered. The sun had not yet risen and the air was cold. A light snow had fallen. It was late November, but they were still wearing the lightweight clothing they'd had on in April. His mother's thin cotton dress was no protection from the frigid air. And he was in shorts.

The officer in charge stood before them. *"Guten morgen."*

Everyone came to attention as the soldiers began the daily head count. No one dared move; they barely breathed. Oscar remembered the soldier who whipped the woman in Szolnok and the guard who threw the coughing woman into the mud. He had seen soldiers lose their tempers for the slightest reasons.

Sometimes these lineups lasted for hours, but this day the roll call was quick. The guard checked off everyone's name and then turned to address them.

"The harvest is over. Today you are being moved."

Oscar felt, rather than heard, the moan that swept through the line. This was the moment they all feared. The farm was safe. Wherever they went next might not be this good. The farmers treated them kindly. There was food and beds.

The crunch of tires broke into his thoughts. Two big trucks rolled to a stop. Fear clouded the air like a wet fog.

At that moment, the farmer and his wife appeared. Each carried a large box. *Is she crying?* The woman, whose name he still didn't know, set the box down in front of him. The farmers were Austrian, not German. They weren't Nazis. They had been kind to the prisoners. They, too, feared the Nazi soldiers, who ordered them around and talked to them as harshly as they did to the prisoners.

The woman stood in front of Oscar. She wore a coat of green wool and a matching hat with a feather. Her expression was somber, but her eyes were kind. "Molasses, from the sugar beets," she said in German and handed him a glass bottle. She looked into his eyes. "Good luck," she whispered. Then she and her husband moved down the row and handed each person a bottle of the syrup.

When all the bottles had been distributed, the soldiers waved the prisoners onto the trucks. Oscar sat on the floor, between Paul and their mother. As the truck left the farm, Oscar saw the farmer and his wife looking after them. Then the truck turned a corner and they were gone.

Chapter 18

Strasshof Concentration Camp, Austria
December 1944

They were transported back to the Strasshof Concentration Camp. Once again, everyone was stripped and hosed down. Only this time the air was so cold that the water felt like ice cubes. By the time they were dressed, Paul was shivering so hard he could barely stand. After their shower they were put into a barrack.

"I'm cold." Paul hugged his chest.

His mother pulled him onto her lap. She rubbed his arms and legs with her hands and then motioned for Oscar to sit beside her. "Lie down on the bed. We'll huddle together to warm each other."

"Anyu, I want to go home." Paul buried his face against her chest. "When can we go home?"

"I don't know, Paul. We must be brave a little longer. Can you do that for me?"

"Yes, Anyu." Paul closed his eyes and was soon asleep.

Like before, they stayed at Strasshof for two weeks. When they weren't lining up for roll call, they were in the barrack trying to keep warm. Then, on December 6, after the morning lineup, they were told they were being moved. And like before, they were taken to the train station and shoved into boxcars.

The inside of the car was freezing. Wind whistled through the cracks in the walls. Paul was crushed between his mother and Oscar, Aunt Bella and the girls crammed beside them.

"Thank God we're all together." Anyu hugged Paul.

"When we get off, hold my hand," Oscar commanded.

"Yes, Oscar." Paul clamped his mouth shut to keep his teeth from chattering. His whole body was shaking.

The train lurched forward and began to move.

Chapter 19

Bergen Belsen Concentration Camp, Germany
December 7, 1944

Paul opened his eyes. The train had stopped. The boxcar door opened and they repeated the now-familiar routine of getting off and lining up. Paul clung to his mother's hand. Oscar was on his other side. The line of prisoners was four deep and stretched as far as Paul could see. Everyone wore the yellow star, so he knew they were all Jewish. No one spoke. The only sounds were the *tramp, tramp, tramp* of thousands of feet, the shouts of guards, and the growls and barks of dogs.

Oscar tightened his grip on Paul's hand. He knew the dogs terrified his little brother. Their eyes glittered with the same hate Oscar saw on the faces of the Nazi guards.

Bang! Oscar jumped at the crack of a gunshot. He knew what had happened—the soldiers had shot some poor person who couldn't walk any more. He grasped his mother's arm and motioned for Paul to hold the other one. *We can't let her fall! We've got to keep her moving!*

They trudged along in silence for several hours. The temperature dropped. Oscar's teeth chattered. His feet were numb. He looked at Paul, whose lips were blue. His brother clutched his heavy molasses bottle to his chest as he walked. One foot in front of the other.

The line stopped moving. Oscar looked ahead and saw a row of low buildings surrounded by barbed wire. A sign said "Bergen Belsen." The line inched forward. When they reached the front, a guard wrote down their names and directed them to the left. Oscar sighed with relief. The guards hadn't taken their molasses, and their families were still together.

✡ ✡ ✡

"Compared to this, our barn was a castle," said Anyu.

She covered her mouth and nose with her hand as she viewed the long room. There was no stove for heat or windows for light. Wooden bunks were stacked three high on both sides of the barrack. The dirt floor and air reeked of filth.

People continued to arrive and soon the room was almost as crowded as the boxcar had been. There were too few bunks, so Anyu and the boys shared a single bunk, and Aunt Bella and the girls took the one above them. Each bunk was a slab of wood with a thin straw mattress.

"Hey, Oscar," said Paul. "Now I can put my foot back in your mouth."

"Very funny." Oscar gave Paul a weak smile, fighting panic. *Now what? What will happen next?*

He didn't have to wait long to find out.

✡ ✡ ✡

"Everyone, out!"

Two soldiers entered the barrack and motioned for them to form a line outside. Paul's breath came out in puffs. He looked at the soldiers, warm in their wool coats, hats, gloves, and leather boots.

A short, stout soldier went from prisoner to prisoner, checking their names off a list attached to a wooden clipboard. When he was finished, he stood back and surveyed the line.

"Look to your left and right. This is where you will stand for the *appel* each morning and night." A female prisoner translated for the soldier. "Everyone must appear for the roll call. No exceptions! You will not leave until you are dismissed!"

Everyone remained standing. They stayed this way for two hours. Guards patrolled the line. Back and forth, they walked, their boots tramping in the mud while the prisoners stood, eyes forward, knees locked, barely daring to breathe. By the time the line was dismissed it had grown dark. They filed back into their barrack. Anyu collapsed onto the bunk. Oscar bent over her.

"Are you all right, Anyu?"

"Just tired."

"Rest, Lenke," Aunt Bella said.

"Yes, I will rest."

"The children need food," Aunt Bella continued. "We have the molasses that the farmers gave us, but we must ration it. We don't know how long we'll be here. Everyone take one sip now and put the bottle away. Then we should all try to sleep."

"It's a miracle the soldiers let us keep it." Anyu unscrewed the cap on the glass bottle and handed it to Paul.

He took a sip. The thick, sticky syrup coated his tongue and throat. "Mmm." He licked his lips. He passed it to Oscar, who took some and then passed the bottle back to Anyu, who hid it behind the mattress. Around them others were settling into their bunks. A heavy silence filled the barrack.

Their first day in Bergen Belsen was over.

Chapter 20

Life in this new camp fell into a harsh pattern.

Every morning, the guards woke the prisoners before dawn and marched them outside, where they stood for hours in the freezing cold. Their teeth chattered; their hands and feet went numb. Yet they stood still as stones because any movement might give the guards an excuse to shoot or to set the dogs on them.

After roll call, they trooped back to their barracks, which were as cold as the outdoors. Twice a day they were fed watery soup made of *duergemuse* (chopped turnips). Paul hated the soup because the turnips were caked with dirt. Other times, the soup contained dirty potato peels. After they ate, Anyu let them have one spoonful each of the molasses.

The winter of 1945 was especially cold. Gusts of icy wind whistled through cracks in the barrack walls. Icicles hung from the ceiling. The only toilets were filthy outhouses. Outside, snow covered the ground, and it seemed that the colder it got, the longer the guards made them stand in the lineups. One day, it was so frigid that Paul started to cry.

"Don't cry!" Oscar hissed.

"I can't help it." Paul sniffled.

"Stop that!" Oscar poked him. "Stand up tall and don't cry!"

A guard stopped in front of them. He looked down at the boys. Paul saw the dreaded SS pin on his collar. His heart was pounding so loudly he thought the soldier could hear it. The guard laughed.

"You scared, little boy? Good. Stay scared." He turned to a boy standing next to Paul. "You look happy today. Why?"

"It's my birthday," the boy stuttered.

"Then you should have a present." The guard removed his pistol from its holster, started to hand it to the boy, and then pulled it back, aimed, and fired. The boy crumpled to the ground as his mother screamed. The soldier whirled around to face her.

"Quiet, or I'll give you the same gift."

Paul looked at the boy on the ground. His stomach heaved; his knees buckled. He was shaking so hard he could barely stand. But he knew he mustn't move or show that he was afraid. Oscar put an arm around him, and they stood in stunned silence until the guards dismissed them and they returned to their barrack.

✡ ✡ ✡

After roll call, they had their meager breakfast. Paul sat on the bed with his plate, but he couldn't eat. He couldn't get the picture of the murdered boy out of his head.

"Why did the soldier shoot that boy?"

"Because he is a miserable excuse for a human," said Aunt Bella.

"These people aren't human," said Anyu. She looked at Oscar and her hand flew to her mouth. "Tomorrow is your birthday," she whispered.

"I'll be eleven," Oscar said proudly. Then his face darkened. "Will the guard shoot me, too?"

"Oscar. We can't tell anyone that it's your birthday. No one. Do you understand?" She turned to Paul. "No one must know!"

"Yes, Anyu." Paul nodded solemnly.

"Kati, Magdi? You will keep this a secret."

"Yes, Auntie Lenke," they chorused.

"No one must know," she repeated, her eyes wide with fear. "Absolutely no one must know!"

For a moment everyone was quiet. Oscar slumped on the bunk, his face in his hands. Paul clenched and unclenched his fists. Anyu covered her mouth, as if stifling a sob. Then she raised her head and took a deep breath.

"Now we must try to forget what happened," she said in a shaky voice. "Come."

She pulled her comb out of her pocket and motioned for the boys to sit beside her. This was their morning routine. First, she used the coffee grounds to wash the boys' hands and faces. Next, she sat, first Paul, then Oscar, on the bunk and combed their hair, picking out lice and nits. She set Paul on her lap and tugged at his hair.

"Ouch! Anyu, you're hurting me."

"Sit still! If we don't remove the nits you'll get sick." Her hand shook as she continued the combing.

Paul yelped and pulled away. "You're mean. Leave me alone."

His mother threw down the comb in exasperation. At that moment a guard stomped into the barrack. "Everyone, outside!" he ordered.

Not again. Oscar sighed. The Germans used surprise lineups to torture them. He looked at his mother. She was weakening. How many more hours of standing in line in the freezing cold could she take?

A sudden thought made his knees go weak.

Do they know that tomorrow is my birthday? he thought. *Are they calling this roll call to shoot me?*

As they walked outside, Anyu gave him a warning look. "Remember what I said," she mouthed.

"Yes, Anyu," Oscar mouthed back. He thought again of the boy, shot dead because he was happy. He looked at his mother, so weak she could barely stand, and at Paul, trying to be brave but actually terrified.

I must stay strong, he thought. *Whatever happens, I must stay strong like I promised Apu.*

✡ ✡ ✡

Every day new transports of prisoners arrived. Sickness and a disease called typhus spread through the camp and hundreds of people died. Food became scarcer. The women often sat together on their bunks, planning meals they would make when they returned home.

"I will make chicken soup floating with schmaltz," said Aunt Bella. "What will you cook, Lenke?"

"I will make goulash with dumplings."

"Ah, I make the best cholent. That is what I will bring," said Sadie, a woman from another barrack who had come to visit.

Paul huddled in a corner of the bunk. All this talk of food made him hungry. It also made him sad because it reminded him of happier times in Karcag. Every Saturday there, Paul,

Oscar, and their parents used to walk to the synagogue for Sabbath services. On the way home, the boys would stop at the bakery to retrieve the pot of cholent, the thick stew their mother left there on Friday evening so it could cook overnight in the baker's oven. At home, they ate their meal, and then Apu and Anyu rested while the boys went outside to meet their friends. Paul thought about holidays at the synagogue, dinners with grandparents, cousins, and friends, and lazy summer days when he and Oscar would ride their bicycles to the Berek, the park with hot springs and a large public swimming pool, on the outskirts of town.

Paul turned to his mother. "Anyu, what does Apu look like?"

Anyu broke off her conversation. "What did you say?"

"I can't remember what Apu looks like."

His mother came over and wrapped her arms around him. "Your father is a handsome man. He has dark hair, like yours, and his eyes are blue, like Oscar's."

"I want to see him."

"I do, too, my darling boy. Soon we will go home and we will all be together and life will be like it was before."

Looking at his stick-thin mother and the other women, whittled by hunger to skin and bones, Paul wondered if Anyu was lying to him. He couldn't believe that life would ever be good again.

Chapter 21

One day after roll call, Anyu grabbed Oscar's hand. For once, she was smiling.

"Uncle Elemir is here."

"What!" Oscar looked around the yard. "Where is he?"

"Over there, in the men's barracks." Anyu pointed to a section on the far side of the yard. "I saw him in the lineup."

"Are you sure it's him?"

"Yes. He recognized us. He waved."

Oscar was happy to know that his uncle was close by, yet he was sad that he was in this awful place, too.

"Let's visit him," said Paul.

"No." Anyu grasped Paul's shoulders. "You are not allowed in the men's camp. Don't even think about going there."

Paul folded his arms across his chest. "I want to see Uncle Elemir!"

"Paul, listen to Anyu," Oscar begged.

"I don't care what you say! I want to see Uncle Elemir!"

"Paul," Oscar snapped. "Listen to Anyu."

Paul frowned. "Yes, Oscar," he whispered and lowered his head so that his brother wouldn't see the gleam of determination in his eyes.

✡ ✡ ✡

That afternoon, Paul waited until his mother fell into an exhausted sleep. Oscar was outside, playing skipping stones with a group of boys. Paul tiptoed in the opposite direction, and when he was out of Oscar's sight, turned and headed for the men's barracks. He was careful not to run because the guards might think he was trying to escape and shoot him. When he reached the barracks, he stopped.

Which of these buildings was Uncle Elemir in? He looked around frantically, afraid a guard might catch him standing there. He brought his hands up to his face. They were shaking. *I have to go back.*

"Paul, come here."

Paul spun around. "Uncle Elemir!" He jumped into his uncle's arms.

"Thank God, you are alive." His uncle set him on the ground. "Who else is here?"

"Anyu and Oscar. Auntie Bella, Magdi, and Kati are with us."

"How are they?"

"Anyu is sick."

"What's wrong with her?"

"She's weak. When we line up, she can hardly stand. Oscar and I hold her up." Paul looked up at his uncle. "Uncle Elemir, how did you get here?"

"By train, how else? You think I was driven in a limousine?" He smiled.

"I mean how did they catch you? Where are Aunt Lily and George?"

His uncle's smile faded. "When I was taken, they went into hiding in a convent. The nuns promised to protect them. I pray they are still safe. I worked in an ammunition factory until the Americans bombed it. Then the Germans brought me here." He placed an arm across Paul's shoulders. "Come, I have something for you."

He took his hand and led him into a barrack. The smell of sickness and unwashed bodies hit Paul like a slap in the face. He noticed that conditions here were even worse than in his barrack. Men lay listlessly in their bunks, their eyes sunk into skull-like faces. Paul shuddered and clutched his uncle's hand. He choked.

"Ah, the hot springs at the Berek this is not," said his uncle, as he rumpled Paul's hair. Then he went to a bunk, reached under the mattress, and pulled out a small knife and a block of wood.

"Come with me." He crooked his finger. "I am going to teach you to whittle."

They walked to a spot at the back of the barrack and sat on a bunk. "We are going to turn this into a horse." His uncle held up a small block of wood. Then he took his pocketknife and began chipping away slivers.

"Uncle Elemir, where did you get the knife?" Paul's voice was filled with awe. The prisoners were not allowed to have tools of any kind.

"I stole it from a guard." He winked. "And the wood"—he pointed to a broken slat in the wall—"I figured no one would miss it."

"Really?" Paul looked at the knife in awe. "Did you fight him for it?"

"Ah, Paul, if only I could have." His uncle shook his head. "No, I had this knife when they took me away. I've kept it hidden." He put his finger to his lips. "So, it will be our secret, yes?"

Paul nodded. Now he had two secrets. The molasses and Uncle Elemir's knife.

"Paul! Here you are!"

Paul looked up as Oscar stormed over to them.

"Look, Oscar. I found Uncle Elemir."

"Hello, Uncle Elemir." Oscar hugged his uncle. Then he turned to his brother. "Paul! Anyu is scared to death. She told you not to come here. How could you run off and frighten her like this?"

Paul folded his arms across his chest. "I wanted to see Uncle Elemir."

Uncle Elemir turned to Oscar. "He is safe with me. As safe as anyone can be in this place," he added under his breath. "So, you are all right?"

"I am not sick. Yet."

"Paul tells me that your mother is ill."

"Yes." Oscar blinked hard.

"Oscar?" Uncle Elemir gave him a questioning look. "Let Paul come visit me sometimes."

Oscar shook his head. "It's too dangerous."

"I'll watch out for him."

Oscar took Paul's hand. "Say good-bye to Uncle Elemir."

Paul waved as Oscar marched him back to their side of the camp.

"Paul, what am I going to do with you?" Anyu frowned at her son.

"I'm bored, Anyu. Uncle Elemir is teaching me to whittle, so I can carve animals out of wood."

"Whittle?!"

"Carving things out of wood." He put his mouth to his mother's ear. "Uncle Elemir has a knife."

"A knife? How can that be?"

"Shh!" Paul placed a finger on her lips. "He keeps it hidden. The soldiers don't know about it. Please, Anyu, let me go see him. I'll be careful."

"Oscar?" she pleaded.

Oscar looked down at his brother. He couldn't blame Paul. The days were endless. With nothing to do, they all spent their time talking, telling each other stories, or just lying on their bunks staring at the bunks above them. But sneaking from their barrack to the men's quarters was dangerous.

"Paul, promise me you'll listen to Anyu."

"*You* sneak out all the time."

"I just hang around outside with the other boys."

"You never let me come with you." Paul pouted.

"I do it to get away from YOU!" Oscar snapped.

"Boys, please. Don't fight." Anyu looked at Paul. "Oscar is right. It's too dangerous to go to the men's camp. Promise me you won't do it."

Paul lowered his head. He bit his lip. "All right. I promise."

And he kept that promise. At least for the next two days.

Chapter 22

February 1945

Paul crept out of his bunk. His mother was sleeping, and Oscar was outside with his friends. Roll call was over and they'd had their bread and coffee. Stuffing his hands into his pockets, he slunk between the barracks where the women and children stayed and walked toward the men's compound. He looked right and left for soldiers and vicious dogs. He was lucky. No one was paying attention to him.

"Uncle Elemir!" he shouted as he burst into the barrack.

"Paul." Uncle Elemir jumped up from his bunk. "Back for another lesson?"

"Yes." Paul pulled the piece of wood he'd taken with him last time from his back pocket. "The horse doesn't have a tail."

His uncle patted his bunk. "Sit." He handed Paul the knife and showed him how to scrape off bits of wood to form the shape of a tail. They worked like this for about two hours. Then he took back the knife.

"You'd better go back. Your mother will be worried." He stood, dusted himself off, and helped Paul up to his feet. "Go! And be careful."

Paul walked back the way he had come. Every few minutes he patted his pocket. Yes, the horse was still there.

When he reached his barrack, Oscar was waiting for him. Paul looked up at his brother and shrugged. Oscar shook his head in resignation.

Paul wanted to be a good boy and listen to Anyu, but sometimes he was so bored he couldn't help himself. He snuck out every day to meet his uncle. It became a game. When he saw a guard, he'd hide, and then when the coast was clear, he'd keep going. He felt bad sneaking out on his mother, but he didn't want to give up the one thing that he liked—his whittling lessons.

But he was always scared. The guards, with their guns and dogs, were huge. He saw prisoners so thin he could count their bones. And garbage everywhere. But when he was with his uncle, he could, for a short time, forget everything that scared him and lose himself in the joy of making an animal out of a block of wood.

Chapter 23

March 1945

There were no radios or newspapers in Bergen Belsen. Yet news managed to seep in. Sometimes they overheard guards talking. Or new prisoners brought information from the outside world. Germany was losing the war. It was just a matter of time before its army collapsed.

"We have to survive until then," Uncle Elemir told Paul. "Tell your mother she must stay strong."

But could she? Paul worried constantly about his mother's health. Then one day, he saw the first spark of real hope.

"Hey, Oscar, look."

Paul was sitting on a pile of rubbish with another boy, staring up at the sky.

"What are you looking at?" Oscar craned his neck. Then he saw it: two planes were buzzing at each other, like bees out of a hive.

"They're German planes. They'll probably drop bombs on us."

"No. One of them is British." The other boy, about Oscar's age, pointed. "See the insignia under its wings? It's a target with red, white, and blue, not a swastika."

"What does that mean?" Paul asked.

"It's a British air force symbol. I saw one before the war. My name's Marek. What's yours?"

"Paul. This is my brother Oscar."

Oscar looked at where Marek pointed. And then he whooped. "You're right! It's a British plane!"

"What is British?" Paul asked.

Oscar looked around to make sure there weren't any soldiers nearby. "The British are people from England who are fighting the Germans."

By now a crowd had gathered around them. Everyone was gazing skyward as the planes swooped and dove at each other, flames spurting from their wings. There was a sudden burst of fire and one plane went spiraling down.

"It's the German plane!" shouted Marek.

Everyone cheered. For a moment they forgot about the guards, the guns, and the dogs.

Two guards appeared. Their hands were wrapped around their guns and they glared at the crowd. "Everyone, back to your barracks. Now!"

They look angry, Paul thought. *Maybe it's because one of their planes was shot down.*

As they trooped back to the barracks, Paul grinned up at Oscar. "Does this mean the war is over?"

Oscar looked at him and winked. "Not yet, little brother, but once the Germans lose…"

Paul looked up at the sky. A wisp of smoke remained where the German plane had been. The rest of the sky was blue.

✡ ✡ ✡

In their barrack, they found Anyu lying on her bunk. When she saw them, she struggled to a sitting position. Oscar told her about the plane fight.

"Whoosh!" he drove his hand through the air. "The British plane swooped down on the Nazi plane and *BAM*, shot it right out of the sky."

"How wonderful." Anyu clapped her hands. "Hooray for the British."

"I saw it too, Anyu. The planes were fighting and fire came out of their wings." Fists curled, Paul pointed his index fingers like guns. "*Bam! Bam! Bam!* Can we go home now?" he asked in a breathless voice. "Can we, Anyu? Can we go home?"

"Not yet, I'm afraid." Anyu pulled Paul onto her lap. "But this gives us hope that the war will end soon." She jumped as a loud voice echoed through the barrack.

"Outside! Everyone! Now!"

Anyu sighed. She motioned for Paul to get up and then struggled to her feet.

"Here, Anyu, let me help you." Oscar took her hand. "I guess the war isn't over yet," said Oscar as they joined the line of people shuffling outside.

"No," sighed Anyu. "Not over yet."

Chapter 24

April 9, 1945

Everyone in the camp knew that Germany was losing the war. Yet in April, they were still prisoners. As the weeks dragged on, conditions in the camp worsened. The Germans had moved thousands of people from other camps into Bergen Belsen. There was barely any food or water. Typhus killed hundreds of people every day.

The first time Paul had gone to visit Uncle Elemir, he had walked past a trench filled with dead bodies. At first he had thought the people were sleeping. But then he had seen the flies and smelled the stink. He had screamed and run away. Every day now, there were more bodies. Some were in trenches; others were stacked in piles. After a while, they didn't frighten Paul. They were just part of life here.

Everyone was waiting for the war to end, for something, anything to happen. Then one day, it did.

"Out, out! *Mach schnell!* Move!"

The guard's voice exploded like a gunshot through the sleeping barrack.

Oscar stumbled to his feet. Paul rolled off the bunk and together they helped their mother. Draping her arms over their shoulders, the boys supported her as they moved to the barrack door. Two guards were stomping up and down the aisle, prodding people who had not responded. A few did not move. Those were the people who had died in the night.

Soon they were assembled outside along with people from several other barracks. It was still dark and the morning air was damp and cold. Paul shivered. Although it was April, it was still chilly and his clothes were little more than rags. As usual, the guards marched up and down the line, checking names on their lists. This time, however, something was different. They were not ordered back into the barracks. Instead, they were told to walk toward the front gate.

It's like when we came here, Paul thought. And then it hit him. *We're going back to the train!*

✡ ✡ ✡

Paul looked up at the boxcar with dread. The thought of once again entering that dark, stinking hole horrified him.

Just as when they arrived at Bergen Belsen, they were forced to walk for miles, this time from the camp back to the train station. Anyu barely survived the walk. How could she survive being locked back into a boxcar?

"It will be all right, Anyu." Oscar tried to reassure her.

"Watch Paul," she said. "Don't let him get lost."

"I'll take care of him, Anyu."

"I won't get lost, I promise," Paul added. The memory of that terrifying time in the Vienna train station still made him shake with terror.

The crowd surged around them, pushing them forward until they were pressed up against the boxcar. Oscar hoisted himself up, and then reached down to help his mother and Paul. Oscar moved them to a corner of the car and settled Anyu on the floor. He sat on one side of her, Paul on the other. He looked for Aunt Bella, Madgi, and Kati but couldn't find them. People continued to pile into the car until there was barely room to stand. Then the door slid shut and, once again, they were plunged into darkness.

Chapter 25

Farsleben, Germany
April 13, 1945

Paul pressed his face to the wall of the boxcar and peered through the narrow space between two boards. They had been locked inside the car for four days. During this time, the train had stopped and started many times. Once a day, the guards would release them from the cars to feed them a watery soup made of potato peels. Otherwise there was no food or water. Conditions had become so bad that it was hard to tell who was alive and who was dead.

"What are you looking at?" Oscar came up behind him.

"S-s-soldiers," Paul stammered.

Oscar peered outside. The soldiers were yelling and setting up machine guns. He closed his eyes. *It's over. They are finally going to kill us.*

"What do you see?" asked a woman behind him.

"Just soldiers," Oscar answered.

"What are they doing?"

"Talking." *Why tell her the truth? She will know soon enough.* Oscar turned away when something caught his attention. What was it? Silence. The guards had stopped shouting. He looked again. *Could it be true?* The soldiers had dropped their weapons and were running away!

"Oscar, where are they going?" Paul asked.

"I don't know."

Other people pressed forward to see what was happening.

"What's that?" Paul peered through the crack.

"It's a tank." Oscar's voice trembled at first and then rose in excitement. "It has a star painted on the front. And there's a Jeep behind it." He turned to face the people huddled behind him. "I think they're American!"

"The guards said that if we surrender to the Americans, the Americans will execute us," said a woman near him.

"I don't believe that," said another voice.

Oscar sucked in his breath. *Are we saved or doomed?* They moved back to Anyu. The inside of the boxcar had become dead silent, as if everyone in it was holding their breath. Outside, they heard voices.

And then, the door slid open.

Chapter 26

Paul stared at the sliver of light at the edge of the boxcar door. It became a wedge and finally opened into a square of brightness. He shaded his eyes and saw two uniformed men standing in the open doorway of the boxcar. One of them put his arm across his mouth and nose. He turned away and vomited.

We must stink. Paul looked down at his ragged clothes and unwashed body, then back at the soldiers. He didn't understand their words but could read their reactions. *They are not going to kill us. They will help us.*

The soldiers were helping people at the front of the car get out. Paul scuttled forward while Oscar stayed with Anyu. When most of the car was emptied, Oscar helped a soldier carry his mother out of the car and settle her on the ground. People were getting out of the other cars, too. Some were wandering about stunned—others were searching for something to eat.

Oscar knelt beside his mother. She was too weak to sit up without his support. He took her hand.

"We are free, Anyu," he said. "The Americans have freed us."

"Thank God." She gave him a weak smile.

✡ ✡ ✡

Paul watched the soldiers as they helped people get off the train. They were different from the Germans. They were gentle. He wished he could understand what they were saying to each other.

He looked around. He was in a field and behind him was a low hill. He saw two boys he knew from the camp. He walked over to them.

"What are you doing?" he asked.

"Eating snails." One boy held up a shell with a curved top.

"I found some matches," said the other boy. "I am making a fire."

Paul joined them. He sat on the ground. Pebbles scratched his bare legs. He took a deep breath. After the stink of the boxcar, the fresh air tasted sweet. One of the boys handed him a snail. The shell was hot and burned his hand.

"I roasted it." He took a twig and dug into the shell. "This is how you get the meat out. Try it." He handed Paul the twig and Paul copied him.

"Yecch." He made a face. Then he laughed. "But it's better than potato-peel soup."

As the trains were slowly unloaded, Aunt Bella and the girls found Anyu. Aunt Bella walked over and sat down beside her friend.

"It's a miracle." Tears rolled down her cheeks.

"Oscar, where's Paul?" Anyu propped herself up on her elbow and looked around frantically.

The Auslander family at home in Karcag after the war in 1947.
From left: Oscar, Lenke, Ignaz, and Paul.

Lenke Auslander died on November 25th, 1951. A year later, due to
strong pressure from the Soviet-controlled communist government
in Hungary, Ignaz decided to change the family name from the
German Auslander to a Hungarian one. They chose Arato.

Ignaz and Lenke Auslander as a young married couple.

Paul Arato (fourth from the left) at the
Zsido Ovoda (Jewish Nursery School) in Karcag in 1942.

The Karcagi Synagogue as photographed in 1981. During their time in Karcag, the family went here regularly for services.

This is the water spigot in Karcag near the Auslander's original home.

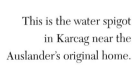

One of the barracks at Bergen Belsen.
Paul, Oscar, and Lenke lived in a building like this while at the camp.

This personnel sheet listed prisoners that arrived at the Strasshof Concentration Camp on July 12, 1944. You can see Oscar, Paul, and Lenke's names on it.

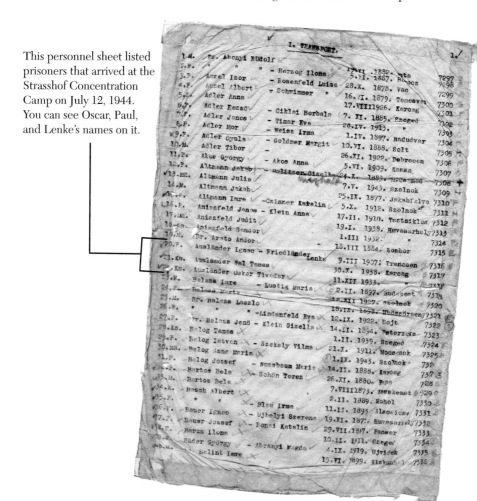

Survivors in a barrack at Bergen Belsen on the day the camp was liberated, April 15, 1945.

A woman and a boy lie on a bunk at Bergen Belsen.

Survivors walk past a massive pile of victims' shoes at Bergen Belsen. These are shoes that were discarded after people were killed.

A woman and her daughter emerge from the death train after being liberated on April 13th, 1945.

A mother and her two sons sit in the sun outside the train after liberation.

Survivors pose after being liberated. The soldier who took this photo, George Gross, was amazed at how quickly they were able to smile after all they'd been through.

Scenes showing the death train from Bergen Belsen on April 13th, 1945, as survivors pour out of it and rest on the nearby hillside.

Fellow U.S. soldiers George Gross (left, the man who took many of these pictures) and Carrol Walsh pose together during the Second World War.

Survivors speak with veteran Carrol Walsh (second from right) at the
American Soldiers/Holocaust Survivors Reunion in Hudson Falls, New York,
September 22, 2009. Paul Arato is far right.

"Give me a hug. You saved my life!" Paul Arato and Carrol Walsh
embrace after meeting for the first time since the liberation.

"I'll find him, Anyu." Oscar left the women and walked to the end of the meadow. They were in a narrow valley. On his right was a hill. He found Paul sitting on the slope with two other boys.

"Paul, what are you doing?" Oscar squatted down beside his brother.

"Cooking." Paul looked up at his brother and grinned.

Oscar wrinkled his nose. "Where did you get the matches?"

"From the train," said one of the boys. He pointed to the deserted engine. "The Germans left them."

"Here, Oscar. Do you want one?" Paul held out a slightly burned shell.

"How can you eat that?"

"I'm hungry," Paul protested. "They taste awful, but I don't care."

"Don't wander off. I don't want Anyu worrying about you. And stop eating snails."

Oscar walked back toward his mother. Halfway there, he paused. The now-empty train stretched like a snake's skeleton along the tracks. *We were inside, waiting to be killed, and now we're free.* He examined his body. The clothes he had worn for the past year hung loose on his thin frame. His skin itched from bug bites, his hair crawled with lice.

None of that mattered now. They were free.

Chapter 27

The tank driven by the soldiers who found the train was huge. Paul craned his neck to see the top. A soldier was sitting in the open hatch. He looked down at Paul and waved. Paul shyly waved back.

The man hoisted himself out of the opening and climbed off the tank. He knelt down. "What's your name, little boy?"

Paul shook his head. He took a step back.

"You don't understand me." The man stood and reached into his pocket and pulled out a candy bar. "Here." He handed it to Paul.

Paul took the candy. It had a brown-and-white wrapper.

"Tootsie Roll," the soldier said. He pantomimed peeling off the paper and taking a bite.

Another soldier walked up to them. He was carrying a camera. He motioned for Paul to join a group of children standing near the hill. He pointed to the camera. Paul shook his head. He smiled at the soldier who had given him the candy and then turned and ran to join Oscar.

"What do you have there?" Oscar pointed to the candy.

"A soldier gave it to me." Paul held it out. "You can have some."

☆ ☆ ☆

Two soldiers were standing nearby. From their expressions Paul could tell that they were angry. *At us?* he wondered.

As if reading his mind, a young woman beside him spoke. "I understand English. They are talking about the Nazis," she said to the boys' questioning looks. "The soldiers say they heard stories about the concentration camps but didn't believe them." She made a sweeping motion with her hand. "Now, after seeing us, they believe everything they heard."

Suddenly, a fleet of army trucks rolled into the valley. Paul grasped Oscar's hand.

"Where are they taking us? I don't want to go."

"Don't worry," Oscar soothed him. "These are the Americans. They won't hurt us."

Paul looked at him, his eyes bright with fear. "How do you know?"

Oscar pointed to the Tootsie Roll still clutched in Paul's hand. "The Nazis never gave us chocolate."

☆ ☆ ☆

"Where are we now?" Paul asked as he leapt from the truck.

"*Fars-le-ben.*" Oscar sounded out the word printed on a wooden signpost. They joined the others from the trucks.

The tall American officer who had opened their boxcar was shouting at a cluster of people—women, children, and a few old men—huddled in the town square. A short man in a dark suit stood in front of him. He was screaming back at the lieutenant. The lieutenant pointed at the townspeople and then at the group from the train.

"What's happening?" Paul asked.

"The man in the suit is the mayor of the town," a woman beside him said. "The American says that the Germans must give us clothes, food, and a place to sleep. The mayor says that we *filthy Jews* are the Americans' problem."

Now everyone was shouting—the mayor, the townspeople, and the lieutenant. Paul watched in fascination as the fight escalated. *The Germans are afraid of the Americans*, he thought. It felt good. And then he gasped. The lieutenant had pulled out his gun and was holding it to the mayor's head. The German's face was so red his cheeks glowed like ripe apples. Sweat dripped from his forehead into his eyes, which switched nervously from the Americans to the townspeople.

"What's he saying now?" Oscar asked the woman.

"The lieutenant says that it was Germans who started the war and they have to make it right—whether they like it or not."

But the townspeople were still protesting. The lieutenant cocked his pistol.

"The American says they have five minutes to cooperate or he will shoot the mayor." The woman smiled. "He wants clean clothes, food, soap, sanitary supplies, and housing, especially for old people and families with children."

Paul held his breath. Would the American really shoot the mayor? While it felt good to see the Americans ordering the Germans around for a change, he didn't want to see the man killed.

The mayor held up his hands. Then he turned to his people and issued orders. The crowd quickly dispersed and the lieutenant put away his gun.

Paul breathed out. He walked over to the army trucks. He watched as soldiers unloaded medical supplies. Suddenly, a wave of panic hit him as he realized he had left his family behind. *I don't want to get lost again.* He looked frantically for Oscar and found him standing with Aunt Bella and the girls.

Then he saw his mother. Two soldiers were carrying her on a stretcher to a truck with a large red cross in its side. They were taking her away! Fear and anger gripped him.

"No!" he shouted. He ran over and grabbed the soldier's arm. "No, no! You cannot take her. You will kill her."

The soldiers stared at him in surprise, clearly unable to understand a word he was saying.

"What the devil…?" said one. He was short and stocky with flaming red hair. "Let go, kid." He looked at Paul's angry face and then shook his head.

"Hey, Bob," he said to his partner. "This kid is terrified. He thinks we're SS and we're going to kill his mother."

"Yeah. I guess he thinks everyone in uniform is evil."

They set the stretcher onto the ground. The red-haired man put an arm around Paul's shoulder.

"We are not Nazis." He spoke slowly and clearly. "We are here to help you. You don't have to be afraid. Do you understand?"

Paul relaxed. For the second time that day, though he didn't understand the words, he recognized kindness and concern in the voice of a soldier. The Americans were going to keep them safe. He bent down and touched his mother's face.

"These soldiers will make you well, Anyu."

His mother smiled weakly. "Where is Oscar?"

"With Auntie Bella, Kati, and Magdi."

"Stay together. Don't wander away."

"I will, Anyu. I promise."

"You are a good boy." She squeezed Paul's hand.
He kissed her cheek and went to join his brother.

Chapter 28

Hillersleben, Germany
April 14, 1945

Paul squirmed on the wooden bench as the truck jounced over rutted roads. Only this time he wasn't afraid, because he knew it was taking him to see his mother. They were going from Farsleben to a town called Hillersleben, where she was in a hospital. Although it was only ten kilometers (six miles) away, the ride was taking a long time because the main roads had either been bombed by the Allies or blown up by retreating German soldiers.

Finally, the truck stopped and everyone got out. Paul looked around. They were standing in a town square. Two other trucks rolled in, followed by a Jeep. The soldiers organized people into lines and brought them to a tent. A woman in an army uniform explained that they would be sprayed with DDT, a chemical that would kill lice.

"At least we're separate from the women," Oscar said, as they stripped and were dusted with a foul-smelling powder. "Yechh." He held his hand over his mouth and nose. "I know we need this but why does it have to smell so bad?"

After the delousing, everyone took a warm, soothing shower. Paul endured the entire delousing process in stoic silence.

"Are you all right?" Oscar looked down at him.

"I want to see Anyu."

"First, we must get dressed." Oscar patted his shoulder. "You wouldn't want everyone to see us naked?"

"No." Paul giggled.

A moment later a soldier appeared with a stack of clean shirts, pants, and underwear, and another soldier brought a box of shoes.

When they were dressed, the boys left the tent. The soldiers directed them to a building that had been turned into a dining room. Aunt Bella, Magdi, and Kati were already there waiting for them.

"You look good, all cleaned up," Oscar teased Kati.

"You do, too." She touched his shirt. "No lice."

They laughed.

"Come, children, let's sit." Aunt Bella ushered them to a table. "It's good to sit at a real table," she sighed.

She smiled up at the soldier who was ladling broth into metal bowls.

Magdi looked up at her mother with big, dark eyes. "Can I have more soup?"

"No. Later, darling." Aunt Bella smiled at her. "Our stomachs have shrunk because of the camp. They can't hold a lot of food. So we must eat slowly and only a little at first."

Paul couldn't believe what was happening. The soldiers treated them with kindness and respect. It was as if he had awakened from a nightmare into a glorious dream. *If only Anyu would get well*, he thought. Now that they were clean and fed, he would ask Oscar to take him to see her.

✧ ✧ ✧

Oscar sat in a chair while Paul perched on the end of their mother's bed.

"Anyu! You won't believe what the Americans did," Oscar began.

"They sprayed us with this awful stuff." Paul held his nose.

"They had to get rid of the bugs." Oscar ruffled his brother's hair. "Look, it's clean."

"It still smelled awful. And they took our clothes and burned them. And gave us new ones!"

"And back in Farsleben, they threatened to shoot the mayor if he didn't get his people to help us! Now Jews are living in the Germans' houses and the Germans are sleeping in tents." Oscar's voice was filled with triumph.

"I know, darling. I *was* there." Their mother leaned back against her pillow. She looked from Oscar to Paul and smiled. "It's good to see you both so clean again. Clean and fed. Where do you sleep?"

"We are in a dormitory. It's where the SS officers used to live. We go to the dining hall for meals. We only eat what they give us." Oscar gave Paul a stern look. "Remember that."

"*Okay.*"

His mother gave him a puzzled look. "*Okay?* What language is that?"

"American." Paul grinned. "The soldiers say it all the time. *Okay!* It means yes!"

"So now you speak American. What else did you get from the soldiers?"

"They gave us chocolate." He pulled a crumpled wrapper from his pocket and extracted a piece of candy. "It's called a Tootsie Roll. And a soldier let me play with his gun."

"A gun!" Anyu gave him a horrified look.

"I told the soldier to take it back. It wasn't loaded," Oscar reassured her.

"The Americans are nice." Paul handed her the piece of Tootsie Roll. "Here, Anyu, this is for you."

"Thank you, my darling boy. This is a miracle. Now maybe God will grant us another miracle and we will find your father."

Paul and Oscar left the hospital feeling better than they had in more than a year. Their mother was still sick, but she was safe and someone was taking care of her.

"I like the Americans," said Paul. Suddenly, he stopped. His face crumpled.

"They're leaving."

Oscar looked to where Paul was pointing. The tall soldier, the one who had rescued them from the boxcar, was sitting in a Jeep behind a line of army trucks. Soldiers were scrambling to get on board as the drivers gunned the motors.

Paul ran over to the lieutenant's Jeep. "I don't want you to go away."

The lieutenant looked at him with a puzzled expression.

"I want you to stay." Paul pointed to the barracks where the soldiers were housed. "Don't go." He shook his head.

The lieutenant got out of the Jeep. He knelt on one knee in front of Paul.

"I know you can't understand me, but you and your brother," he pointed to Oscar, "are going to be fine." He patted each boy on the head. Then he cupped Paul's chin in his hand. "*You are going to be fine,*" he repeated, saying each word slowly.

Paul nodded. He didn't understand the words, but he reacted to the kindness in the lieutenant's voice. "Thank you," he said in Hungarian.

"Thank you," Oscar echoed.

"Good." The lieutenant stood and brushed off his pants. He smiled at the boys, saluted them, and then got back into his Jeep. His driver put it in gear. Then one by one, the American soldiers who had saved their lives left the town.

"I will miss them," said Paul.

"Me, too," said Oscar

Sixty years later, Paul would remember that moment and how he thought he'd never see the soldiers again.

Chapter 29

Hillersleben, Germany
May 7, 1945

"Anyu, it's over. The war is over!"

Oscar ran into the ward, where the doctors and nurses were clustered around a small radio. The British prime minister, Winston Churchill, was speaking. Although he could not understand the words, Oscar recognized the note of triumph in the prime minister's voice. When the speech was over, a nurse translated it for them.

"Mr. Churchill said that the war will end one minute after midnight tonight. He says that we should let ourselves rejoice, that in all of England's history, there has never been a greater day than today."

The patients, nurses, and doctors all cheered. Oscar bent down to kiss his mother.

"Where is Paul?"

"Playing soccer." Oscar grinned. "Don't worry, Anyu, the older boys are taking good care of him." He paused. "Now that the war is over, we can go home."

He looked at his mother and his spirits sank. In the three weeks they'd been in Hillersleben, many of the patients had recovered and left the hospital. Anyu, however, was still too weak to be moved. Whereas others were slowly gaining weight, she remained thin. The dark circles around her eyes had disappeared, but her skin was pale. Oscar thought of his father. When would they be able to go look for Apu?

Oscar kissed his mother good-bye and walked out to the town square. Soldiers were slapping each other on the back, laughing, and a few were even singing while the German citizens of Hillersleben watched silently.

At first, Oscar felt sorry for these people, mostly women and children, huddled together looking sad and defeated. Then he remembered Bergen Belsen and the train. He thought of the people who had died and those, like his mother, who might never recover. He remembered the cruelty of the German guards: the snarling dogs, the dark, putrid boxcars.

You started this war, he thought. *You created all this misery.* Turning his back he walked away from the square and headed to the edge of town to find his brother.

They stayed in Hillersleben while Anyu recovered in the hospital. Oscar and Paul slept in a dormitory with Aunt Bella and the girls. New survivors and orphaned children arrived, searching for their families. Relief workers aided those people who wanted to leave Europe and live in countries such as America and Canada.

Whenever someone left for one of these countries, Oscar felt a stab of jealousy. He liked the American soldiers who had rescued them. He thought it would be good to live in a country with such wonderful people. But there still was no word of Apu or Aunt Bella's husband, Chaim. Anyu and Aunt Bella wanted to return to Hungary to find them.

Chapter 30

"At least we're in passenger cars this time."

Oscar looked out the train window at the passing countryside. He saw farm fields with cows grazing, chickens pecking the dirt, and the occasional pig, rolling in mud. They passed villages, many of them little more than piles of rubble. A boy pedaled alongside the train on a bicycle. He took off his cap and waved. Oscar waved back.

"We're still being watched by soldiers." Kati's voice broke into his thoughts.

"The Russians aren't as nice as the Americans or British, but they're nicer than the Nazis," said Paul.

"At least they are taking us home." Oscar turned to his mother. "Aren't they, Anyu?"

"Yes, darling." She gave him a weak smile.

As Oscar turned back to the window he thought about what had happened since their liberation. In the end, they had stayed in Hillersleben for four months—their mother remained in the hospital the whole time. In August, the British, who had replaced the Americans, had turned all the Hungarian refugees over to the Russian army. The Russians were now in charge of people from Eastern European countries, including Hungary. They put them on a train for Budapest.

Although they were in a passenger train, conditions were far from good. The train moved slowly, stopping often to let troop trains go by or to wait for a damaged bridge to be repaired. Food was whatever the Russians could scavenge from people along the way. There was no place to bathe and only one toilet for each overcrowded car. *But we are going home.*

Oscar's body convulsed with a wracking cough. His mother looked at him with a worried expression.

"Oscar, your cold is getting worse."

"I'm all right, Anyu." Oscar tried to stifle another cough, but it forced its way out.

Anyu sighed. "At least Paul is fine."

"I am fine, too, Auntie Lenke," said Kati. She was seated across from them, between her mother and Magdi.

"Thank God." Anyu rested her head against the back of the seat and closed her eyes. Just then the train squealed to a stop.

"Another delay," Aunt Bella grumbled. "Will we ever get home? The war has been over for five months but we are still wandering around Europe like lost souls."

Oscar pulled down the window and stuck his head outside. The train had stopped in the middle of a village. Three Russian soldiers were arguing with a group of women. One of them pointed to a badly damaged house. Most of the roof was gone and the windows were shattered. The soldier snapped an order. The woman turned and ran to the house, returning a few minutes later with a basket filled with bread, a fat round sausage, and some apples. The other women, who had scattered at the soldier's command, returned with similarly filled baskets, which the soldiers took before jumping back on the train.

Oscar turned away from the window. Anyu had fallen asleep. Paul was curled up on the seat with his head in her lap. Aunt Bella had also dozed off. Kati and Magdi were playing a clapping game. He wrapped his arms around his chest. *No more coughing*, he told himself. *I have to be strong so I can help find Apu.* He closed his eyes and let the rhythm of the train rock him to sleep.

Chapter 31

Budapest, Hungary
September 1945

"Anyu, where are they taking us?" Paul asked.

A woman in a white uniform was helping his mother into an ambulance. They had arrived in Hungary after three grueling weeks on the train, where they were met by a team of aid workers.

"Where are we going?" This time Paul asked the woman supporting his mother's arm.

"The Jewish hospital," she said. "Your mother is sick and so is your brother." She turned to Oscar. "The doctor will see about your cough."

"We want to go home to Karcag to find our father," said Oscar.

"And I suppose that cough is my imagination," the woman said, as Oscar doubled over. The nurse motioned him into the ambulance. "You, too, young man." She smiled at Paul.

"But I'm not sick."

"No, but you can't stay in the railroad station by yourself, can you?"

Paul shivered. He still remembered being lost at the Vienna train station. "No, ma'am," he said and meekly climbed into the vehicle.

✡ ✡ ✡

"Why do they have to take out my tonsils?" Paul demanded.

"It's the only way they can keep you here," said Anyu. She was lying in a bed in the hospital, with Oscar in the bed next to her. Paul stood between them.

"I don't want them to take out my tonsils!"

"They'll give you ice cream afterward," said Oscar. He propped himself up on his elbow. "You like ice cream, don't you?"

"Chocolate ice cream?"

"If that's what you want." A nurse smiled down at him. "Now, be a good boy. I promise you will be fine."

✡ ✡ ✡

What good is ice cream if your throat aches so much you can't eat it? Paul looked down at the dish holding a chocolate puddle.

"Anyu, my throat hurts," he croaked.

"It will be better soon," she soothed. "Look how strong Oscar is getting."

"I'll eat the ice cream if you don't want it." Oscar walked over to Paul's bed.

"No!" Paul clutched the dish. "It's mine."

Anyu laughed. "See, you're not really so sick. Maybe tomorrow Nurse Koltai will let you go outside to play. If you are well enough to eat your food."

Paul looked at the sunshine streaming through the window. "I'd like that." He lifted the spoon to his mouth.

Chapter 32

I made it! Paul climbed to the top of a pile of rubble. Budapest had been heavily bombed and there were piles of debris everywhere. One especially large pile sat in front of the entrance to the hospital. It was Paul's favorite spot to play. Here he could climb to the top and pretend he was a soldier spying on the enemy. At other times, he would sit at the base and use pieces of debris to build structures such as houses or forts. Today, he and his friend Tommy were searching for Nazis.

"Hi, Tommy. Up here."

"Whew." Tommy wiped his face with his sleeve. He was wearing short pants and his knees were scratched. "We're on top of the mountain!" He crowed. "Now we can shoot at the bad guys."

Paul pried a steel rod from between two slabs of stone and pointed it like a gun. *"Bang, bang!"* Then he stood up and shaded his eyes with his hand.

"Do you see any more soldiers?" Tommy asked.

"Not yet." Paul turned. "We should hide. In case they come looking for us."

"Wait!" Tommy held up a hand. "I see one!"

"Where?"

"There." Tommy leaned over the edge of the pile and pointed up the street. He picked up a chunk of cement. "Arm yourself!"

Paul didn't answer.

"Paul, I said arm yourself."

Paul still didn't answer.

"Hey, are you all right?" Tommy grabbed Paul's arm.

Paul wrenched it away. He turned and raced down the pile, tumbling the last few steps and landing on his hands and knees. Lurching to his feet, he ran toward the approaching figure.

"Apu," he cried, waving his arms. "Apu!"

The man stopped and stared.

"Paul!" he shouted. He moved toward him and lifted him in the air. "Paul!" He crushed his boy against his chest. He set him down and then kneeled and examined him. He touched Paul's face, ran a hand over his hair, and then cupped his chin in his hands. "You are all right?"

"Yes, Apu." Paul looked up at his father. "I couldn't remember what you look like but then when I saw you I recognized you."

His father wiped his eyes. "Yes, Paul, we recognized each other."

"Anyu is worried about you," said Paul.

"Where is she? And Oscar?"

"They are in the hospital. Come." Paul took his father's hand. "I'll take you to them."

✡ ✡ ✡

116

Paul entered the ward, pulling his father forward. "Anyu, Oscar, look! Look who I found outside! I found him! I didn't forget him after all!"

Anyu opened her eyes. She blinked, stared, blinked, and stared again.

"Ignaz?" she said in a voice filled with disbelief.

Her husband walked to her bed and took her hand. Then he turned and looked at Oscar.

"You are all alive. Thank God." His voice broke.

"When did you get back?" asked Anyu.

"Chaim and I got back to Karcag in August." Apu sat on a chair between the beds. Paul sat on his lap. "We escaped from the Germans with five other men."

"How did you do that?" Oscar's voice was filled with awe.

"We waited until the guards were sleeping..."

"Did they all sleep at once?" Paul asked.

"Of course not, stupid." Oscar rolled his eyes. "If they all slept, then they wouldn't be guards." He turned to his father, eyes wide. "So what did you do?"

"Did you kill them?"

His father didn't answer.

"Did you, Apu?" asked Paul.

"Let's just say that we did what we had to do."

"You *did* kill them. Good!" Oscar clapped.

"Oscar, stop badgering your father."

"What happened next, Apu?" Oscar asked, ignoring Anyu.

"When we escaped, we were still in Russia. We didn't know where we were and had no idea how to get back to Hungary. So we hid in the forest for six months."

Oscar was impressed. "Where did you hide?"

"In the trees. In holes in the ground. Under piles of leaves. Anywhere we could."

"What did you eat?" asked Paul

"Nuts, berries. Sometimes we even got some food from friendly farmers."

"You mean you stole food." Oscar grinned.

"Sometimes." His father shook a finger at Oscar. "You are asking *too* many questions."

"But you still haven't told us how you got back to Hungary," said Paul.

"Ah, that was lucky. By then it was December. The weather was freezing, and it was getting harder and harder to find food. Just when we thought we couldn't survive much longer, we met a group of Russian soldiers." He shook his head. "At first they thought we were German spies. They were going to shoot us."

"Ignaz!" His wife clapped a hand over her mouth.

"How did you convince them that you weren't spies?" Oscar bounced up and down in his seat.

"One of the soldiers was Jewish. We spoke to him in Yiddish. Once we convinced them that we were Jews, they took us with them. So we came into Hungary with the Russian army." His smile faded and his voice became serious. "When we got to Karcag, we found out that everyone had been taken away. We have been waiting for you to come home. Then Bella arrived yesterday and told me that you were here."

Oscar was happy to see that some color had returned to his mother's cheeks. Her eyes shone with a glimmer of light. His father looked older. His hair was flecked with silver, his face filled with lines that had not been there before the war.

Suddenly, the excitement he had felt over his father's escape faded.

"Apu," he said, his voice shaking, "who else came back?"

His father lowered his head. "People are still returning."

"Did Grandpa and Grandma come home?" asked Paul.

Apu covered his eyes with his hand. "Not yet. We will wait and hope. In the meantime, I will talk to the doctor and arrange to take all of you home."

Home? Will Karcag still feel like home? Not for the first time, Oscar wondered what they would find and, more importantly, *who* they would find. He looked at Paul and his parents. The four of them had survived. That was a miracle. But he wanted everyone to come home.

He fought back tears. Throughout their ordeal he had never cried and he wasn't about to start now.

Paul was sitting on his father's lap. Now he turned and looked up at him. "Apu, when I saw you outside, I recognized you." His voice was filled with wonder. "I couldn't remember what you looked like. And then I saw you and I did."

Chapter 33

Karcag, Hungary
November 30, 1945

Oscar sat in the kitchen of the house Apu had rented. Their original home had been bombed, so Apu had arranged to lease the house of a family who had not returned. *The Szabos were our friends. They're dead and now we're living in their home.* Oscar shuddered. As he had feared, only a fraction—about 200 of the town's 1,000 Jews—had survived.

Oscar found it strange that the adults expected everyone to carry on as if nothing had happened. *It's as if we fell asleep and woke up to find our friends and family just disappeared.* After their father brought them home, Oscar noticed that the younger children, like Paul, seemed to recover. But he wondered if they really had or if they were just hiding the same anger and pain that he felt. As for the adults, they went about their daily routines grimly. No one spoke about the Germans or the camps. No one mentioned the people who were gone. *I used to have grandparents. I used to have aunts and uncles and cousins. Why don't we ever talk about them?*

"Oscar." Paul bounced into the kitchen. He held up a large piece of wood. "I found this outside. I'm going to carve it into a top, like Uncle Elemir taught me."

Oscar smiled at his brother. Their uncle had also survived and returned to Budapest, where he'd found his wife and son with the nuns who had risked their lives to hide Jews in their convent.

"I'm going to show Anyu." Paul walked to the bedroom where their mother was resting. While others had regained their strength, their mother had remained weak. The doctor said it was because of the typhus she had contracted in Bergen Belsen.

At that moment the door opened and Apu walked through the front door.

"Oscar, take this." He handed him a large pot. "Aunt Bella made us soup."

Oscar took the pot and set it on the stove. It was still warm. He took bowls and spoons from the cupboard and placed them on the table. Anyu stepped into the living room with Paul by her side. Tonight was the first night of Hanukkah. Anyu had set out a menorah—a candleholder with nine branches—beside a pair of Sabbath candlesticks.

"First, we will light the Hanukkah candles," she said.

"I forgot about Hanukkah. What is it?" Paul asked his father.

"On Hanukkah we celebrate that 2,000 years ago a group of Jewish freedom fighters called the Maccabees won a battle against Antiochus, the Greek king of Syria who outlawed the Jewish religion. He decreed that Jews must worship Greek gods."

"I know the rest of the story," said Oscar. He turned to Paul. "After they won, their leader, Judah Maccabee, wanted to rededicate the Temple but there was only enough oil to light the menorah for one day. Then a miracle happened."

"I know! I know!" Paul clapped his hands. "The oil lasted for *eight* days."

"That's right." Their father beamed at them. "And that's why we light our menorah every night for eight nights." His voice became serious. "Oscar, help Paul light the first candle.

As the boys lit the candle, the family chanted the holiday blessing. Then Anyu lit the two Sabbath candles, covered her face, and recited the blessing. When she lowered her hands, Paul saw tears in her eyes.

"Anyu's coming with us to the synagogue." Paul held his mother's hand and guided her to the table.

"Are you feeling better, Anyu?" asked Oscar.

"Much better, Oscar." His mother sat in the chair he held out for her. "Thank you for helping Apu."

"Anyu, you look pretty." Paul said to his mother as they ate their soup.

"It feels good to be in new clothes." She straightened the collar of her dress. It was red with white dots. The color gave her cheeks a rosy glow. "And you boys look handsome in *your* new clothes." She smiled. "It's so good to see you clean and properly dressed."

"The people from America have been very generous," said Oscar.

Boxes of food and clothing from the United States had been arriving every week. Slowly, life was returning to the way it had been before the war. *Except for the people who didn't come back.* Oscar remained quiet until they finished eating and Apu said it was time to go to the synagogue.

✡ ✡ ✡

As they walked up the road toward the synagogue, they met friends and neighbors. Everyone said *"Gut Shabbes,"* Yiddish words that meant "Good Sabbath." Children scampered ahead of their parents, calling greetings to each other. Oscar searched the street and saw a girl with red hair up ahead. He recognized her as his friend Sarah from school. He wove through the crowd and caught up with her just as she reached the synagogue steps.

"Sarah!" He grasped her arm.

"Oscar!" Sarah turned and threw her arms around him. "You're safe."

"You, too. I was so worried. When you weren't here I thought…"

"We were in a displaced persons camp in Germany. We just got back."

"I–I guess we should go inside." Oscar smiled shyly. He linked his arm through Sarah's, and they walked into the synagogue.

As they entered, Oscar looked around. The first thing he noticed was the broken windows. Next was the sulfur-colored stain on the front wall where someone had thrown eggs.

"It's not too bad…considering," a woman behind him said.

"Considering what?" said her companion.

"Considering that they could have bombed the building, like they did our houses."

"Eggs they threw. Better they should have eaten them."

Oscar and Sarah looked at each other. She giggled.

"I have to go up to the women's gallery."

"Let's walk home together after the service."

She nodded.

Oscar looked around for Paul. He was with a group of children at the front. A man was handing out blue-and-white flags with the Star of David on them. *No more yellow stars*, he thought. The children waved the flags in the air, shouting and laughing, while several adults tried to calm them down. Finally, the children went to their seats, boys downstairs and girls in the gallery. The rest of the congregation became quiet as Mr. Gross got up to speak.

"*Shalom.*" His voice cracked. "Tonight, we celebrate the beginning of Hanukkah. It's appropriate that we should do so tonight because, in a way, we are rededicating our synagogue... thanks to Reverend Papp, who has brought us a very special Hanukkah present."

He signaled to two men behind him to open the doors of the ark. There, nestled in the wooden cabinet, were three Torah scrolls, each encased in a dark blue velvet cover and embossed with a golden Star of David.

The congregation gasped.

"I thought the Germans destroyed the Torahs," Oscar said to his father.

"They would have, if they had found them," Apu replied. "Reverend Papp rescued them and hid them in the bell tower of his church. The Germans would have arrested him if they knew."

"Why did he do it?" Oscar asked. He remembered how the townspeople had watched in silence as their friends and neighbors were loaded into trucks. He recalled passersby outside the brickyard where Jews were being herded onto railroad cars—going about their daily chores as if nothing was happening.

"Why did the reverend risk his life for us?"

"He's a good man," said Apu. "There *are* still good people, Oscar." He nodded at the podium where Mr. Gross was welcoming the reverend.

The priest was a tall man, clean-shaven with thinning brown hair and a kindly face. He stood, his hands on the lectern, and looked down at the congregation. His gaze was strong, his smile warm.

"*Shalom*, my friends," said Reverend Papp in an emotion-filled voice. "Welcome home."

Chapter 34

Toronto, Canada
Spring 2009

Paul took a deep breath, blinked hard, and tried to steady his nerves. Despite his initial hesitation, he had finally written to Matt Rozell, the New York state teacher who had posted the pictures of the train—*his* train—on the internet.

In response, Matt had written this back:

> *Dear Paul,*
> *Please contact Frank Towers. He has all the information about the liberation and the soldiers who were involved.*
> *Paul, meet your rescuer.*
> *All the best,*
> *Matt Rozell*

Now, Matt was organizing a reunion. Paul would meet the soldiers who had liberated him. For almost 65 years he had thought about the train. Had things really happened the way he remembered? He'd been so young. Were there two soldiers on a tank or one in a Jeep, or both?

He remembered that the Americans had given him candy. *It was a Tootsie Roll*, he recalled. *Another soldier let me play with his gun. That totally freaked out Oscar and my mother.*

He smiled. *For so many years, I've searched for information about that train.*

And now here it is.

✡ ✡ ✡

Since liberation, Paul's life had taken many turns. His mother never recovered from her illness and died in 1951, when he was thirteen. Three years later, his father married Olga, a woman from their town. Although the Germans were gone, they continued to suffer under a cruel dictatorship. After the war, Russia occupied Eastern European countries, including Hungary. These countries were said to be "behind the Iron Curtain," because their citizens could not leave.

The Russians closed Jewish schools in Hungary, so Ignaz Auslander started teaching in a public school. The Russians had many rules—one was that anyone holding a public position, such as a teacher, had to have a Hungarian name. Auslander was German, so in 1952, Ignaz chose the name Arato—it started with an "A," was short, and was easy to spell.

In 1956, Paul and his brother were living in Budapest when public resentment against the government erupted into a violent revolution. Fed up with tyranny and war, they joined thousands of refugees and fled the country. They escaped at night by crossing fields studded with landmines. Once free, they went to England and then to Canada. Oscar eventually settled in Australia, but Paul remained in Toronto.

Even as he struggled to suppress his wartime memories, Paul suffered their effects. Except for his father and Oscar, his whole family had died. His father stayed behind in Hungary. In Canada, he met other Hungarian refugees, but, at first, no one would talk about their experiences during the war. There was no one with whom to share the deep-seated feelings of anger, sadness, and fear that haunted him.

Then, suddenly, thirty years after liberation, people began talking about what was now being called the Holocaust. There were reminders everywhere—in books, movies, on television, and in the stories survivors were beginning to tell. Still, Paul kept silent. Except about one story: how he was liberated from a train by American soldiers.

Paul wanted to thank the soldiers for what they had done for him and his family, but he knew there was no way to find them. And then, one day, he read an article about Americans liberating a train in Germany. As he looked at the accompanying pictures, he began to shake. *I was on that train. I recognize the valley where it's stopped.* His heart pounded.

Do I want to reopen the wounds?

Can I live with the memories that will come back?

The answer, he finally decided, was "Yes."

Chapter 35

Hudson Falls, New York
September 2009

Matt Rozell stood in the hotel lobby waiting for the first participants to arrive. After six months of planning, the symposium was about to begin. Tonight was the opening reception. He turned to an older gentleman—a veteran—standing beside him.

"We have seven survivors coming. It's a wonderful response."

"I never thought I'd see any of these people again," the vet said.

At that moment, another man walked up to Matt. They greeted each other warmly. Then Matt turned to the vet.

"Carrol Walsh, this is Paul Arato. One of the train survivors."

Paul threw his arms around Carrol. "Give me a hug," he said in an emotion-filled voice. "You saved my life!"

✡ ✡ ✡

The sign over the door said: "Americans Came to Liberate, Not Conquer."

Paul walked into Hudson Falls High School the morning after the reception, more nervous than he could ever remember being. How would he react to the stories of other survivors? Would he be able to tell his own story without breaking down? Had he made a mistake in coming?

The students had turned the hallway into a World War II museum with photos of soldiers, battles, and the pictures that a soldier named George Gross had taken on the day of liberation. Maps were marked with the route that the 9th Army followed on their trek across Europe.

Paul studied the display. "This is amazing."

He walked up to the registration desk. A student smiled up at him. "You're a survivor, aren't you?" She looked at Paul in awe.

"Yes." He smiled back at her. He thanked her and took his registration materials.

"Don't forget this." She handed him a green wristband that read: "Remember the Holocaust—end prejudice and hatred." Paul looked around and saw that everyone was wearing one. It felt good.

For the next two days, Paul and his wife, Rona, mingled with survivors, students, teachers, and representatives from the National Holocaust Centre in Washington, D.C., and historians from the Bergen Belsen Museum in Germany. They listened to testimonies from soldiers—including Frances Curry, who won a Congressional Medal of Honor for saving the lives of seven soldiers—and from train survivors. He mixed with teachers and students. He talked, laughed, cried, and celebrated life in an atmosphere of joy mixed with sadness.

As speaker after speaker made their presentations, the kids hung on to every word. Soon, it was Frank Towers's turn to speak—the same Lieutenant Towers Paul had said good-bye to in Hillersleben all those years ago.

As Frank walked onto the stage, the audience fell into respectful silence. At 93, he was still an impressive figure. Standing over six feet tall, his face radiated warmth and sharp intelligence.

"For weeks," he said, "we had heard stories of German atrocities against Jews and dismissed the stories as propaganda." He fixed the audience with a knowing gaze. "Then we found the train and we believed."

Carrol Walsh spoke next. Carrol, who was 88, had a youthful smile and a twinkle in his eyes. But when he started talking, his expression turned serious.

"When George and I first saw the train we couldn't believe our eyes. And the smell! We opened the boxcar doors and the stink almost knocked us over." He paused and looked out at his audience. "The survivors have thanked us for rescuing them, but they shouldn't. They don't owe us a thing. We owe them. For what we allowed to happen to them."

Both men received standing ovations from the audience. It was now Paul's turn to tell his story. His knees shook as he walked from his seat onto the stage. When he reached the podium, he took a deep breath to steady himself. He began:

Hello and my heartfelt greetings to all of you. I feel honored to have been invited to this symposium. As you heard from Mr. Rozell, I am a survivor of the Bergen Belsen Concentration Camp and of the death train, which was liberated by Carrol Walsh, George Gross, and Frank Towers's 30th division of the U.S. 9th Army. I came to this symposium to meet my liberators and to thank them for giving me a second chance at life. I'm going to be brief, but I do want to tell you how I got to Bergen Belsen.

I was born a long, long time ago in a place far, far away—in Karcag, a small town in Hungary, somewhere between Budapest and the Ukrainian border. When I say that I came from a place far, far away, I mean that I hope that the Karcag of 1938 stays far, far away. By God, I hope it remains something that none of you nor my children or grandchildren ever have to know. The Karcag of 1938 was a segregated place, with a Catholic boys' school and girls' school; a Protestant boys' school and girls' school, and a small Jewish school with two teachers, one of them my father. In the Hungary of 1938 my father was only allowed to teach Jewish children, just as Jewish doctors could only attend to Jewish patients.

As you might know, newly born Jewish boys are circumcised at eight days. My father told me that I was circumcised on the day when, throughout Germany, windows and doors of Jewish homes and businesses were smashed, synagogues were burned, people were beaten and many killed. We remember that day as Kristalnacht. During the next seven years, most of the Jews of Europe were murdered. You have studied what happened during the Holocaust and have heard stories from my fellow survivors about Bergen Belsen. So let me fast forward.

As you are witnessing here, some of us survived those years in spite of it all. Like my fellow survivors, along with my mother and brother, I was liberated by these brave, wonderful, and fantastic soldiers. While I was too young to remember their faces, I never forgot the men. This symposium is a tribute to these brave and wonderful soldiers and to the many others that fought and died in battles. And on a personal note, while the men of the 30th Division were storming the beach at Normandy, Sam Rimler, my future father-in-law, was spotting shellfire on a barge 500 meters from shore.

Matt Rozell told me that there might be as many as 800 students, teachers, and visitors here this week and it might be overwhelming. In spite of his warning, I wouldn't want to be anywhere else in the world right now. I think I am speaking for all my fellow survivors when I say that in one form or another, we relive every day some of those horrors of 65 years ago. How could anybody forget having seen his mother's suffering? No six-year-old should ever have to witness his beautiful 37-year-old mother—who gave him life, sustained him, and looked after him—suffer in those terrible circumstances, her health deteriorating to the point where she had to be carried off of the boxcar at the time of liberation.

So why would I still want to be here and publicly relive the horrors of the Holocaust? It sounds insane! The answer is: you, my audience. *You are the third generation since WWII and you are caring and have the courage to share those horrors with us. And for that, I salute you! And so, we owe you to be here and share it with you.*

In closing, I want to salute the America which produced the soldiers of WWII and of all the wars before and since, and which is still producing decent young people today. It reinforces my gratefulness and love for America.

May God Bless America and my thanks to you all.

The audience jumped to its feet. Paul looked out at a sea of young people. They were cheering, clapping, and crying.

I have reached them, he thought. *I have touched their hearts and their minds.*

He stepped down from the stage and went into the audience to greet his newfound friends.

✡ ✡ ✡

On Friday night, the survivors, soldiers, teachers, and students who had worked on the program gathered in a restaurant overlooking Lake George for a closing dinner. Matt had learned that afternoon that Diane Sawyer of ABC News was featuring the Symposium for her weekly "Person of the Week" segment. Over a hundred people crowded the restaurant's lounge, where a large screen television was tuned to ABC. The mood was buoyant as they watched reports of the week's happenings. Then, as the special segment began, everyone became respectfully quiet.

This story takes place in the closing days of World War II, as American and British forces pushed into Germany from the west and the Soviet Red Army closed in from the east...

When the piece ended, the room erupted in cheers. Everyone rooted like kids at a football game. Paul and Oscar had been two of the children rescued from that train. As the group stood and moved into the dining room, Paul thought of the strange set of coincidences that had brought him here—a teacher's desire to make history relevant to his students; a newspaper article that his son, Daniel, had stumbled upon on the internet.

And tonight, the journey that began in heartache and terror 65 years earlier was concluding with peace, hope, and love.

Author's Note

I met Paul in 1967. He had graduated from Art Center College of Design and was working as a toy designer for Mattel Toys. I was teaching sixth grade, so dating a toy designer was cool—a perfect fit. After visiting Israel, I had spent three months backpacking through Europe. On our first date I showed Paul pictures from my travels. One was of the Anne Frank House in Amsterdam. Paul looked at it and said, "We were in the same camp." I was stunned to realize he didn't mean a summer camp. He meant the Bergen Belsen Concentration Camp.

Paul and I were married in 1968. What I didn't realize at the time was that I was marrying the Holocaust as well. Even though he rarely spoke of his wartime experiences, it was always with us—in the way his mood would suddenly darken, in his nervous tension that never went away, or in his explosions of temper, like the time he shouted at an usher in a movie theater because the boy waved his flashlight and ordered us to line up against the wall.

Paul had never told his story to our three children, Alise, Debbie, and Daniel. In 1995, I became an interviewer for the Survivors of the Shoa Visual History Foundation, the project that Steven Spielberg founded to record stories of Holocaust survivors. I thought that interviewing other survivors would help me understand Paul. I eventually convinced him to be interviewed and it was by watching his interview tape that our children finally learned his story, including his liberation by the U.S. 9th Army. When Daniel found the article Matt Rozell had posted called "The Train near Magdeburg," he sent me an email: "Mom, read this article and then show it to Dad." I immediately recognized that this was the train from which Paul and his family were rescued.

At first, Paul was reluctant to contact Matt. He didn't want to open old wounds. But I convinced him to send Matt an email. Once he did, and Frank Towers answered him, Paul couldn't wait to meet his liberators.

The men of the 30th Infantry Division belong to what is called "The Greatest Generation." These soldiers, along with all the Allied forces, fought to save the world from tyrants who would destroy our freedoms. They landed on the beaches of Normandy, fought ferocious battles in France, Belgium, and Germany. Yet they never lost their humanity. When they came upon a train filled with ragged, starving concentration camp survivors, they stopped and did not move on until every person from that train was fed, clothed, housed, and for those who needed it, had received medical attention.

It was by chance that Matt Rozell learned of their story. The program that he started as a simple high-school history project continues to grow and has changed his life and the lives of those it touches. In 2009, the National Society of the Daughters of the American Revolution chose Mr. Rozell as the New York State Outstanding Teacher of American History, and in 2012 he received their highest national education award, the Mary Smith Lockwood Founders' Medal for Education. In 2010, he was selected by United States Holocaust Memorial Museum to participate in the National Days of Remembrance ceremonies at the U.S. Capitol Rotunda with General David Petraeus and 171 American soldier liberators to commemorate the 65th anniversary of the end of World War II. In 2011, Mr. Rozell traveled to Israel with Frank Towers and met over 65 survivors, and hundreds of their family members, whose lives have been affected by this project.

In telling this complex story, I have used the facts as they were related to me by the people who lived it. I had the privilege of listening to the testimonies of soldiers and survivors at the Hudson Falls symposium and at two other reunions that Paul and I have attended. I've read many books and articles about the events of that dreadful time and the 115 interviews I conducted with Holocaust survivors gave me an all-too-vivid picture of what these people had to endure.

When writing a historical novel, however, one must sometimes fill in the gaps. The scenes are the way Paul and others described them to me. The dialogue is what I believe they would have said. Though these are not their exact words, I hope I have captured their truth. The Auslanders, Feins (Aunt Bella, Magdi, and Kati), Uncle Elemir, Matt Rozell, and the U.S. soldiers are real people. The characters of the Nazi guards are based on what I have read and been told.

A Note about the Exchange Camps and the Last Trains

Three trains left Bergen Belsen between April 6 and April 11, 1945. They were the last transports out of the camp before it was liberated by British soldiers on April 15 and, together, these trains carried about 6,700 people.

Although they didn't know it at the time, these prisoners were a part of a group of over 20,000 Jews that Adolf Eichmann agreed to "put on ice" so they could be exchanged at some point for food, money, or German prisoners of war. They were deported to Strasshof, and then sent to work as slave laborers in factories and on farms.

In December 1944, 4,200 Hungarian Jews—those who had worked on farms—were sent to Bergen Belsen. They were housed in a section fenced off from the rest of the camp, known as the "Hungarian Camp." Another larger, similar section—the "Star Camp"—had Jews from other countries who were to be exchanged. Paul had always wondered why the SS allowed them to keep the molasses that the farmers gave them. Now we know that conditions in these exchange camps were slightly better than in other sections. Children up to the age of 14 stayed with their mothers, and prisoners were allowed to wear their own clothes and keep their possessions.

Only a few hundred prisoners from those camps were actually exchanged. The rest ended up on the three trains. One train delivered its Jewish cargo to the Theresienstadt Concentration Camp, where survivors were liberated on May 8, 1945.

Another train seemed to drop off the map. It left Bergen Belsen on April 11 and spent two weeks zigzagging through Germany in an effort to avoid the approaching Allied armies. It was freed by the Russian army in the small German town of Tröbitz on April 23. Of the 2,700 people on that train, over 600 died during the trip and after liberation.

The train that the Auslanders were on left Bergen Belsen on April 9 and was liberated by American troops near Farsleben, Germany, on April 13. For over fifty years, copies of the pictures that George Gross took that day remained in a shoebox in Carrol Walsh's closet. After his interview with Matt Rozell, he found them and Matt posted them on his website. George Gross had said that what impressed him the most when he took the pictures were the brave smiles of the newly liberated children. In his own words:

I was assigned to stay overnight with the train, to let any stray German soldiers know that it was part of the free world and not to be bothered again. I was honored to shake the hands of the large numbers [of survivors] who spontaneously lined up to introduce themselves and greet me in a ritual that seemed to satisfy their need to declare their return to honored membership in the free society of humanity.

That ritual was repeated—this time with hugs and tears— over six decades later when survivors and soldiers reunited at the symposium in Hudson Falls High School.

Acknowledgments

Writing this book was an emotional journey. My husband, Paul, allowed me to share his story, even though it meant reliving a painful part of his life. He became ill while I was working on it and passed away three months after it was published. However, he shared my commitment to the project and was proud to attend the book launch. During the writing, his brother Oscar passed away, but I know that he too gave his blessing to the book.

To Matt Rozell, all I can say is that you, too, are a hero. What an amazing job you have done bringing this story to light and to life. To the men of the 30th Infantry Division, bravo! You were heroes then and you are my heroes today. You helped save the world from a vicious regime and you did it with courage, humility, and a caring that continues to inspire us all. And a special thanks to Carrol Walsh, who brought this story to light, and Frank Towers, who continues to search for train survivors that he calls "his children."

To the survivors of the train near Magdeburg, I salute you. You have endured the worst that life can throw at you and you have not only survived, you have thrived. Among your number are doctors, lawyers, university professors, child psychiatrists, engineers, teachers, and an industrial designer. You have raised families and now enjoy the love of your children, grandchildren, and even some great-grandchildren. And that, as Paul says, is the best revenge of all.

My special thanks go to the team at Owlkids. From the start of this project, you have been encouraging and supportive. Through many revisions (I've lost count), name changes, and title changes you have continually assured me of the importance of this book. To my editor, John Crossingham, you have given me insightful advice and moral support and stayed calm, even when I demanded to know why we needed another rewrite. My publisher, Jennifer Canham, has been a rock of encouragement throughout. I want to thank the Ontario Arts Council for its support while I was writing this book.

Special thanks to the Gross family for allowing me to use their father's photos. They capture in a way that no words can the emotions of that unforgettable day. And my thanks to the researchers at the United States Holocaust Memorial Museum and to Elizabeth Banks for their valuable assistance.

And to my amazing children—Alise, Debbie, and Daniel— you have lived this story most of your lives. Growing up as children of a Holocaust survivor is not easy, but you have taken pains to learn about your father's background and give him the love and support to deal with it. And, of course, you have given us both the best gifts of all—three gorgeous grandchildren—Cy, Samantha, and Tali. May they and their children and grandchildren grow up and live in a world where Holocausts do not happen.

About the Author

Rona Arato is an award-winning author and a teacher. She was born in New York and grew up in Los Angeles, where she attended UCLA and earned a BA in Education. She lives in Toronto and is a dual American and Canadian citizen. Rona began her writing career while her children were growing up. From 1994–1998, she interviewed Holocaust survivors for Steven Spielberg's Survivors of the Shoa Visual History Foundation, an experience that helped her understand her husband's background as a Holocaust survivor. Rona has since turned her attention to writing books for children, with a focus on human rights.

Photo credits